THE FORMATION OF
THE NEW TESTAMENT

THE FORMATION OF
THE NEW
TESTAMENT

H. F. D. SPARKS

SCM PRESS LTD
56 BLOOMSBURY STREET
LONDON

First published 1952

Printed in Great Britain by
Northumberland Press Limited
Gateshead on Tyne

TO
THE MEMORY
OF MY MOTHER
BLANCHE BARNES SPARKS
(7 APRIL 1872 – 2 JUNE 1951)
WHO
HAD SHE LIVED
WOULD HAVE RECEIVED
THE ROYALTIES
FROM THE SALE OF THIS BOOK
AND
THROUGHOUT THE PERIOD
OF ITS COMPOSITION
WAS WONT TO REFER TO IT
AS
'MY BOOK'

CONTENTS

TO THE READER

I SHOULD not have thought of writing an introduction to the New Testament if I had not been invited to do so for a series. After I had finished the book, circumstances made it necessary for me to withdraw it from the series, and from the publisher who first commissioned it. So it now appears as an independent study and under the auspices of another publisher, to whom I am naturally more than usually indebted.

The book claims to be no more than a simple introduction, designed for the reader who is beginning the subject. If it has one special merit, that merit is that it does at least try to present the literature of the New Testament against its historical background and to relate it to the life of the Church.

H. F. D. SPARKS

The University
Edmund Street
Birmingham, 3
2 June, 1952

PROLOGUE

IT HAS been often and aptly remarked that the New Testament is 'the Church's Book'. And this remark will serve as a convenient indication both of our immediate point of departure and of our future line of approach.

But what do we mean by 'the Church's Book'?

There are many who understand the phrase to mean no more than that the New Testament is the book above all others which the Church *possesses*. For them the New Testament is a unique and priceless collection of sacred literature, given to His people by God Himself. From it the essence of Christianity may be derived: from it the truths of traditional Christian doctrine may be established; and to it any private participant, or any ecclesiastical party, may appeal with justification in any conceivable controversy. On this view, the New Testament is the Church's authoritative text-book in matters of faith and morals.

With the general idea expressed in this view there is obviously no need to quarrel. The trouble is, however, that it does not go nearly deep enough. For the every-day practising Christian it is doubtless adequate. It may even be adequate for the professed theologian, for the moralist, for the apologist, and perhaps for the ecclesiastical historian. But for the student of the New Testament itself it is clearly not adequate. For him the New Testament is 'the Church's Book' not so much because the Church has for centuries *possessed* it, as because the church originally *produced* it. And here we must remember that the Church produced the New Testament in two quite distinct and separate ways.

In the first place, the Church produced the New Testament in the sense that the individual books were written within the bosom of the Church and to satisfy the needs of the Church. The writers, of course, had no intention of writing Scripture—if they had they would in all probability have written very differently. Nor in the main, so far as we can tell, had they any serious literary ambitions. They wrote rather as Christians writing for their fellow-Christians: to instruct, advise, admonish, exhort, or comfort, wherever the need might be.   And whatever use may have been made of their writings later, and whatever significance attached to them, this primary fact must never be forgotten.   The books of the New Testament were written one and all by members of the earliest Christian communities to meet particular situations and emergencies which arose within those communities.   They were in origin neither Scripture nor Literature, but the natural and inevitable product of the growing infant Church.

Yet the Church produced the New Testament not merely in the sense that the Church's needs and difficulties were responsible for the writing of the individual books.   The Church produced the New Testament also in the sense that it was the Church that defined authoritatively what books the New Testament should contain and what books it should not.   The idea of a New Testament (i.e. a collection of specifically Christian sacred writings that could be placed alongside the sacred writings of the Old Testament inherited from Judaism, and be regarded equally with them as the Word of God) seems to have originated during the second century. But immediately the question was raised, Which of the many Christian writings in existence can legitimately be termed 'sacred'? And which, in consequence, ought to be included in the new collection?   Although there was general agreement about some books almost from the first, about others opinions differed; and it soon became clear that no ultimately satisfactory answer could ever be given on the basis of purely individual or local preference.   The matter was one which could be decided only by the Church corporately.   As it happened, Christians had to wait for more than two hundred years before the final decision was reached.   But in the end that decision was a corporate decision of the universal Church.

Thus, for the student of the New Testament itself, it is first and foremost 'the Church's Book' because both in its separate parts, and as a whole, it owes its origin to the Church.   This fact will accordingly condition our approach.   We shall not approach the New Testament from the theological angle: that is, we shall not start by treating it as a God-given unity, and then go on to treat one by one the contents of the individual books—though to do so

would, of course, be not only right, but also essential, in certain
other contexts. Instead, our approach will be historical. We shall
take as our starting-point the origin, growth, and development of
the primitive Christian Church; after which we shall try, so far
as we can, to fit the books of the New Testament into their appropriate places in the story. This will occupy the first and the four
succeeding chapters, in which we shall see how the devotional and
social life, the organization, the theology, the day-to-day needs, the
questionings, and (be it remembered also) the quarrels, of the
Church produced books differing widely both in form and content.
And then, in a final chapter, we shall sketch the stages by which
the twenty-seven books that make up the New Testament to-day
alone became recognized throughout the Church as together con-
stituting an authoritative scriptural ' Canon '.[1]

[1] On the origin and meaning of the term ' Canon ', see below, p. 149.

Chapter One

THE PRIMITIVE CHURCH
AND ITS GOSPEL

CHRISTIANITY started its career as a small and despised sect within Judaism. To the outside observer at the time there would have seemed no essential difference between this new 'sect of the Nazarenes'[1] and the many other Jewish parties. So, at least, it appeared to the Roman procurator, Festus, even as late as the year 56. For him the points at issue between St. Paul and his accusers were no more than 'certain questions of their own religion'.[2] And there is no doubt that Festus was right. To begin with all Christians were Jews. Such differences as there were were differences in interpretation of the religion received from their forefathers—more precisely, differences in interpretation of the age-old Jewish hope for the future, which the upstart 'heretic' Christians would persist in asserting in the teeth of their 'orthodox' Jewish opponents was in process of being fulfilled.

An understanding of this hope for the future is therefore of cardinal importance if we are to understand the nature of primitive Christianity.

'In the beginning,' the Scriptures affirmed, 'God created the heaven and the earth':[3] God had also created man 'in his own image'.[4] And this belief in the creative activity of God was the basis of Jewish thinking. But man, through his sin in the Garden of Eden, had marred the divine image in which he was created, and had been in consequence condemned to a life of toil and suffering.[5] Yet from the mass of fallen humanity God had chosen one man, Abraham;[6] and He had promised to his descendants a great and glorious future.[7] From their temporary bondage in Egypt He had redeemed these descendants as 'a peculiar people unto himself':[8]

[1] Acts 24.5. [2] Acts 25.19. [3] Gen. 1.1. [4] Gen. 1.27. [5] Gen. 3.17-19.
[6] Gen. 12.1-3. [7] Gen. 15.6; 17.4-8. [8] Exod. 19.1-6; Deut. 7.6.

15

He had led them forth and settled them in Canaan, ' a land flowing with milk and honey';[9] and He had subsequently given them a king to rule them as His own personal representative.[10] In view of his status as God's representative, and the special ritual act by which he was consecrated, the king was repeatedly referred to as ' the Lord's Anointed '[11]—in Hebrew *mašiah* or ' Messiah '. More-over, David, the second king, was promised that his dynasty would be permanent.[12]

But whatever might be the theory, permanence and stability seemed in practice the very last things to be achieved. The land itself did not fulfil expectations. Nor did the kings that succeeded David. And rarely for more than a few years together was there any peace or security from the attacks of warlike neighbours. Then came the crowning disaster of the exile. Even so, there was no quenching of the spirit. Far away in Babylon some, at least, of the captives still hoped for the fulfilment of God's promises and waited patiently for the day of deliverance. When it came and they were restored to their own land once more, it was only natural that they should think that the promised age of blessedness had now at length arrived; and that they should see in the prince Zerub-babel a ' branch '[13] of the house of David, their divinely ' anointed ' king.

Again, however, their hopes were doomed to disappointment. The returned exiles were now part of the Persian Empire. And their Persian overlords, though kindly disposed in many ways and prepared to allow considerable freedom, were certainly in no mood to countenance any nationalist aspirations. To the Persians suc-ceeded the Macedonians: to the Macedonians the Ptolemies: to the Ptolemies the Seleucids; and then finally, in the year 63 B.C., the mighty power of Rome. Things had gone from bad to worse. It was not God's land, so it seemed, that His people lived in, but a land controlled by aliens: it was not the rule of ' the Lord's Anointed ' that they acknowledged, but the whim of a foreign despot. Some acquiesced in this state of affairs and fared outwardly very well. Others took refuge in a purely individual and inward piety. Nevertheless, though necessarily driven underground, the hope for the future never died. Instead, it underwent a transforma-tion.

[9] Deut. 26.8,9; Josh. 24.17,18.   [10] I Sam. 10.24; 12.13.   [11] e.g. I Sam. 16.6; 26.9.
[12] II Sam. 7.12-16.   [13] Zech. 3.8; 6.12; cp. Isa. 11.1 and Jer. 23.5; 33.15.

Broadly speaking, we may say that the hope was transferred from the terrestrial plane to the celestial. The present world, it was asserted, was too bad, much too bad, ever to become the scene of the fulfilment of God's promises. Indeed, it was so bad that God Himself had no intention of allowing it to survive much longer. Suddenly, in His own good time, He would intervene, wind up the existing order, and destroy what once He had made. And just as 'in the beginning' He had created the world that now is, so 'in the end' He would create another to take its place—a new, more perfect, and more glorious, world, where all would be perpetual righteousness, and joy, and peace. 'For behold,' declared a prophet in the name of God, 'I create new heavens and a new earth, and the former things shall not be remembered nor come into mind.'[14]

The time of God's intervention was referred to as 'the Day', a phrase first found in the Old Testament in Amos.[15] 'The Day', it was popularly believed, would be heralded by signs and portents, which no one who had been properly instructed beforehand could fail to recognize. Then, when it actually dawned, this present age would be brought to an end through a universal natural catastrophe: a great Judgement would follow immediately, in which the wicked would be condemned; and the new age would at last be inaugurated, wherein God's people would enjoy unhindered a life of everlasting bliss.

Because this new age was to be established by God's final victory over the powers of evil, and because its chief characteristic was to be His unfettered, permanent, and universal, sovereignty, it soon became generally known as 'the Kingdom (or Reign) of God'. From the statements of the older literature it is clear that the majority thought that when the Day came God Himself would appear as Judge, and that He Himself would be the Ruler in the Kingdom that was to follow.[16] Later, however, it was more usually expected that He would act through an intermediary. And just as in days long ago He had ruled Israel through His 'anointed' king, so, similarly, it was thought He would both inaugurate His Kingdom in the future, and rule it, through a specially appointed 'anointed' agent—i.e. His 'Messiah'.

There are a number of available descriptions of the nature and functions of the Messiah in the later literature. And from the wide divergences that these descriptions exhibit it is plain that the

[14] Isa. 65.17.　　　　[15] Amos 5.18.　　　　[16] e.g. Isa. 65.17-25; Joel 3.9-21.

B

Jews achieved even less unanimity in their ideas about the Messiah than in many other matters. For our purposes, however, it will be sufficient simply to note without comment three of the more important titles applied to the Messiah in this literature—viz. 'the Son of David', 'the Elect One', and 'the Son of Man'; and to conclude our summary by quoting a few specimen verses from Enoch as a convenient illustration of one, at any rate, of the popular versions of the hope:

(i) *The Pre-Mundane Appointment of the Messiah*

'And at that hour the Son of Man was named
    In the presence of the Lord of Spirits . . .
Yea, before the sun and the signs were created . . .
    His name was named before the Lord of Spirits.'[17]

(ii) *The Judgement*

'On that day mine Elect One shall sit on the throne of
    glory,
    And shall try men's works.'[18]
'Downcast in countenance shall the kings of the earth
    become,
    And the strong who possess the land . . .
As straw in the fire so shall they burn before the face of
    the holy:
As lead in the water shall they sink before the face of the
    righteous,
    And no trace of them shall any more be found . . .
For they have denied the Lord of Spirits and His
    Anointed.'[19]

(iii) *The New Heavens and the New Earth*

'And I will transform the heaven and make it an eternal
    blessing and light:
And I will transform the earth and make it a blessing:
And I will cause mine elect ones to dwell upon it:
    But the sinners and evil doers shall not set foot
    thereon.'[20]

[17] Enoch 48.2,3.   [18] Enoch 45.3.   [19] Enoch 48.8-10.   [20] Enoch 45.4,5.

(iv) *The Messianic Kingdom*

'And in those days the Elect One shall sit on my throne,
    And his mouth shall pour forth all the secrets of wisdom
        and counsel;
For the Lord of Spirits hath given them to him and hath
    glorified him.
And in those days shall the mountains leap like rams,
    And the hills shall skip like lambs satisfied with milk . . .
And the earth shall rejoice, and the righteous shall dwell
        upon it,
    And the elect shall walk thereon.'[21]

Such, in barest outline, was the Jewish hope for the future, which was the basis of Christian theology. At first, the only difference between Jews and Christians was that whereas the Jews still looked to a vague and indefinite future and for a Messiah as yet unknown, the Christians claimed that the hope was already in process of fulfilment and that they knew who the Messiah was, namely, the Jesus they had known and loved on earth.

The fulfilment of the hope and the Messiahship of Jesus were in consequence the two main elements in the primitive ' Gospel ', or ' Good News ', as it was first proclaimed. Acts gives us several epitomes of early sermons;[22] and although, of course, these epitomes are very far from being shorthand reports of the words actually uttered on any particular occasion, there is no sound reason for doubting their substantial accuracy. It is, therefore, to them that we must now turn in order to discover in greater detail the content of ' the Gospel '.

First, the speech of St. Peter on the day of Pentecost, epitomized in Acts 2.14-40. The tiny band of Christians, we must remember, were suddenly called upon to justify their admittedly very strange behaviour. This behaviour, St. Peter explained, was due not to drunkenness as some had maliciously suggested, but to the out-pouring of the Spirit of God. Long ago the prophet Joel had fore-told this outpouring as one of the signs of the coming of ' the Day '. Joel's prophecy was now fulfilled. But there was another, and

---

[21] Enoch 51.3-5.
[22] Acts 2.14-40; 3.12-26; 4.8-12; 5.29-32; 7.2-53; 10.28-43; 13.16-41; cp. also 4.24-30 and 8.30-38.

more important, set of facts to consider. All present would be familiar with the main events of the life of Jesus and with the circumstances of His death. God had clearly set the mark of His approval on the life of Jesus because through His agency He had allowed miracles to be wrought. He had equally clearly set the mark of disapproval on those who had crucified Jesus because He had subsequently raised Him from the dead. Some might deny the Resurrection. Yet St. Peter and his friends were witnesses that it had actually happened: it had also been foreshadowed by David in the Psalms. Moreover, God after raising Jesus had exalted Him to the heavens, in this way plainly indicating His Messianic office. And now, according to His promise, He had poured out His Holy Spirit as all could see and hear. Let them, therefore, ponder the true significance of what had happened. Let them admit that 'the Day' was near. Let them acknowledge that Jesus was indeed Messiah. And let them turn and be baptized as an outward sign of that acknowledgement, so that they too might escape the perils of the Judgement and receive as well the gift of the Holy Spirit which was available to all.

The next example is another sermon of St. Peter, delivered to the admiring crowd immediately after the healing of the lame man at the Temple (Acts 3.12-26). The healing of this man, St. Peter asserted, had not been brought about through the power or righteousness either of himself or of his companion, St. John. It had been accomplished solely through the power of the name of Jesus acting through them as human agents. Jesus was God's 'Servant', about whom Isaiah had written in the later chapters of his book; and, as Isaiah had foreseen, He had been rejected and killed by His own people, the Jews. God, however, had reversed their verdict, and by the Resurrection had glorified Jesus. No doubt the Jews had acted in ignorance. They now had a chance to retrieve their mistake. Let them examine the Old Testament and see for themselves how not only the advent of Jesus, but also His suffering, had been foretold: let them repent and have their sins forgiven; and let them prepare themselves against the appointed hour when Jesus would appear from heaven in His true glory as Messiah. By so doing they might hope, as Abraham's faithful heirs, to enter upon that inheritance which at the very beginning of their national history God had covenanted to give to Abraham's children—the unlimited and lasting blessings of the Messianic Age.

As our final example may be cited the epitome of St. Peter's message to the Roman centurion, Cornelius (Acts 10.28-43). That St. Peter, a Jew, should unhesitatingly enter the house of Cornelius, an 'unclean' Gentile, when to do so was strictly forbidden by the Jewish law, is explained as due to a direct divine revelation. St. Peter had been expressly warned to call no man 'unclean'. He had been made to realize that God was 'no respecter of persons' and that He accepted the worship of a faithful and righteous Gentile exactly as He accepted the worship of a faithful and righteous Jew. For anyone brought up in Judaism this was, of course, a new departure. Yet it was all part of God's eternal purpose, now openly declared in the Christian 'Gospel'. This 'Gospel' centred on the person of Jesus, who, as was well known, began a public ministry soon after the close of the ministry of John the Baptist. The mighty works of Jesus in healing the sick and suffering were sufficient proof that 'God was with him'; and His own immediate followers were witnesses of everything, not only of His works of healing and His later shameful death, but also of His Resurrection, after which they had been specially commissioned to preach that He was 'ordained of God to be the Judge of the living and the dead'. The prophets too were witnesses of what St. Peter now proclaimed, that through the Name of Jesus everyone that believed in Him, whether Jew or Gentile, would receive remission of his sins.

Perhaps it may be objected that this last example, in so far as it introduces the new element of the inclusion of Gentiles within the Church, cannot fairly be adduced as evidence for the content of the *primitive* Gospel. The objection has some force. Yet it is precisely for this reason that the account of the Cornelius incident is worth special attention, since it shows clearly that at least until the Gentile Mission was fairly launched upon its course, whatever an individual preacher might believe to be the implications of the Gospel, and in whatever new situations he might be called upon to proclaim it, its essential content still remained the same.

This content we may now summarize as follows:

(1) God had chosen Israel as His people and through the patriarchs and prophets had promised them a glorious future; but they had always been rebellious and rejected the prophets whom He sent.[23]

(2) Finally God had sent Jesus, whose life and works were facts

[23] On the rebelliousness of Israel see especially the speech of St. Stephen (Acts 7.2-53).

of recent history; but they had also rejected Him by condemning Him to death.

(3) God, however, had reversed this verdict through the Resurrection, which had been alike witnessed by His followers and foreshadowed by the prophets.

(4) Indeed, the extremely close correspondence between the whole series of events connected with Jesus and what the prophets had foretold would happen in the times of the End proved conclusively that God was at last fulfilling His promises, that the Day was about to dawn, and that Jesus was Messiah.

(5) Therefore, let those who heard admit the soundness of this interpretation: let them repent and be baptized; and so, with the gift and guidance of the Holy Spirit which they would receive through baptism, let them await in quiet confidence the return of Jesus on the clouds of heaven to inaugurate the Judgement and the new age which was to follow.

At first there was no open breach between Christians and Jews. The Gospel was, as we have seen, fundamentally Jewish; and the primitive preachers made no attempt to separate themselves from the established observances of Judaism. Although, naturally, they met 'at home' for prayer and their own peculiar rite of 'the breaking of bread',[24] they still continued to frequent the Temple and synagogues as they always had.[25] They had no idea whatever either of being, or of becoming, separatists. Rather did they regard themselves as the most faithful of faithful Jews; for to them alone of all the Jews God had granted an understanding of the purpose of His work in Jesus, and had in addition commissioned them to proclaim the fulfilment of the Jewish national hope.

Official Judaism, however, took a different view and was antagonistic from the start.[26] Then St. Stephen became involved in acrimonious discussion with certain Jews of the Dispersion (i.e. Jews whose homes were outside the boundaries of Palestine).[27] They preferred a charge of blasphemy against him, and secured his condemnation and execution. A general persecution followed. And from now on the gulf which the Jewish authorities had always realized divided them from the Christians began to widen. As a result of the persecution the little community in Jerusalem was

[24] e.g. Acts 1.14; 2.42,46.   [25] e.g. Acts 2.46; 3.1; 9.2,20.   [26] Acts 4.1-11.
[27] Acts 6.9,10.

'scattered abroad throughout the regions of Judaea and Samaria';[28] while some even 'travelled as far as Phoenicia, and Cyprus, and Antioch'.[29] Inevitably they took the Gospel with them; and in this way it reached a far wider public than it could have done had there been no persecution.

But the contact with a wider public only widened the gulf still more. In Jerusalem it had been accepted as axiomatic that the Gospel was a message of 'Good News' for Jews and no one else: God had made His promises to Israel, and only those who were genuine Israelites could hope to inherit the promises. Yet outside Jerusalem and its immediate neighbourhood this axiom began to be questioned. What of the Samaritans, for example, who, although not recognized by official Judaism, none the less had some claims to consideration in as much as they too traced their descent from the same forefathers as the Jews and accepted the Law of Moses? What, again, of the many 'God-fearers', who, although of Gentile birth, had been admitted by the Jews themselves to a sort of associate-ship in Judaism and were allowed to share in Jewish worship? What, even, of the despised Gentiles who had no connection with Judaism at all? Were God's promises really limited to the Jews? Might it not be that as a consequence of their deliberate rejection, first of their own prophets, and then finally of Jesus, the Jews had forfeited their exclusive rights as heirs to the promises? Might it not be that God's purpose was more extensive, and that all mankind, whether Jews or not, were destined to share in the fulfilment of the promises, if only they were prepared to accept the Gospel?

These questions, of course, did not present themselves in the first instance as purely theoretical possibilities. They arose as the outcome of practical experience. After the 'scattering abroad' which followed St. Stephen's martyrdom St. Philip, finding himself in Samaria, preached so successfully to the Samaritans that St. Peter and St. John went specially from Jerusalem to set their seal upon his work; and as they were returning they too 'preached the Gospel to many villages of the Samaritans'.[30] St. Philip, subsequently, received a divine command to evangelize and baptize a God-fearing Ethiopian who was on his way home from worship in the Temple;[31] and immediately afterwards extended his mission to 'all the cities' of the maritime plain between Azotus and Caesarea.[32]

---

[28] Acts 8.1   [29] Acts 11.19.   [30] Acts 8.5, 25.   [31] Acts 8.26-39.
[32] Acts 8.40.

Later, we find St. Peter also active in this district;[33] and, once more by divine command, a God-fearing Roman, Cornelius, together with his household, was admitted to the Church, having received the Holy Spirit before even he was baptized—a manifest and incontrovertible sign that God Himself approved.[34] At Antioch, where the local church was founded by converts from Cyprus and Cyrene, the preaching was designedly to Gentiles[35] as well as to Jews; and the success of this new departure was likewise regarded as a sign of divine approval.[36] And then St. Paul and St. Barnabas embarked from Antioch on a mission to Cyprus and Asia Minor, which, owing to the comparatively poor response of their Jewish hearers, soon assumed a predominantly Gentile character.[37] Yet in spite of these developments it is safe to say as a general rule that throughout this early period the acceptance of non-Jewish adherents was due not so much to deliberate policy as to the compelling force of circumstances. Any preacher outside Judaea was bound to find among his audience a high proportion of non-Jews, and the fact that so many of them so regularly responded with such eagerness was equally bound to be taken as conclusive evidence that God had ' touched their hearts '.

Such a broadening of the basis of Church membership, however, was not allowed to pass unchallenged. The older Christians of Judaea were seriously disturbed. When they heard of the Cornelius incident they accused St. Peter of ' going in to men uncircumcised and eating with them ' and thereby contravening the Mosaic Law, which all Christians, it was assumed, were under obligation to observe. It was only when St. Peter had explained that he had done what he had in obedience to a direct command of God, and had further stressed the special manner in which Cornelius had received the Holy Spirit and its resemblance to their own experience at the day of Pentecost, that they withdrew their charge and were driven to admit that ' to the Gentiles also hath God granted repentance unto life '.[38]

Even so, the matter did not end there. The majority maintained that although Gentiles might legitimately be received into the Church, it was essential that they should submit to the rite of circumcision and also accept as binding all the other ordinances of

---

[33] Acts 9.32-43.   [34] Acts 10.1-48.
[35] There can be no doubt that the reading ' Greeks ' (i.e. pure Gentiles) in the R.V. at Acts 11.20 is right as against ' Grecians ' (i.e. Jews of the Dispersion) in the A.V.
[36] Acts 11.20-24.   [37] Acts 13 and 14.   [38] Acts 11.1-18.

the Law. In other words, a Gentile in order to become a Christian must become a Jew as well.

The controversy came to a head soon after St. Paul's return to Antioch from his journey in Asia Minor. 'Certain men,' we are told, 'came down from Judaea and taught the brethren, saying, "Except ye be circumcised after the custom of Moses, ye cannot be saved".' Such an assertion contradicted the ideas of St. Paul and of the Antiochene church as a whole; and a deputation was sent, with St. Paul at its head, to take council with 'the apostles and elders' in Jerusalem about what might rightly be required of Gentiles when admitted to the Church. The upshot was a decision adverse to the circumcisionists. 'It seemed good to the Holy Ghost and to us,' the decision ran, 'to lay upon you (i.e. the Gentile Christians) no greater burden than these necessary things; that ye abstain from things sacrificed to idols, and from blood [, and from things strangled],[39] and from fornication; from which if ye keep yourselves, it shall be well with you.'[40]

And by that decision the gulf between the Christians and official Judaism was deepened far more than it was widened. It was now a gulf which no power on earth could bridge.

We have dealt with the beginning of the Gentile Mission in some detail, not merely because it is something of paramount interest and importance in itself, but also because it influenced the presentation of the Gospel in a variety of different ways.

For example, the influence on the titles applied to Jesus. The primitive preachers had proclaimed Jesus as 'Messiah' and had in consequence habitually applied to Him the subsidiary Messianic titles—'Son of David', 'Son of God', 'Son of Man', 'the Man', 'the Servant of the Lord', and 'Lord'. All these titles were derived either from the Old Testament or from other Jewish sources, and naturally Gentiles found them strange and often meaningless. As a result, in predominantly Gentile churches the generic title

---

[39] In most authorities for the text of Acts the decision is concerned with both ethics (i.e. the prohibition of idolatry and fornication) and ritual (i.e. the prohibition of 'eating with the blood', or, as we say to-day, eating meat not slaughtered in the approved 'kosher' fashion). But in some authorities the words 'and from things strangled' are omitted. If these latter authorities are right all possible traces of Jewish ritual requirements will have been allowed to disappear. The decision then must be understood as concerned with ethics only—i.e. the prohibition of idolatry, murder, and fornication, to all of which vices Gentile converts might have been expected to be especially prone.

[40] Acts 15.1-29.

'Messiah' soon lost its primary theological significance and came to be employed in its Greek form 'Christ'[41] as a proper name. Of the subsidiary titles, the more distinctively Jewish (i.e. 'Son of David', 'Son of Man', 'the Man', and 'the Servant of the Lord') dropped out of use almost entirely, and attention was concentrated on 'Son of God' and 'Lord', which had meaning for both Jew and Gentile. The first of these, 'Son of God', had in Judaism a very respectable pedigree as a Messianic title, being derived ultimately from God's promise to David in II Sam. 7.14: it was also applied in Gentile circles, sometimes to the ruling Roman Emperor, and sometimes to the wonder-working prophets that were to be met with all over the Graeco-Roman world.[42] Similarly, 'Lord' was a familiar title for Jesus in the primitive Christian communities of Palestine:[43] but it was also used by Gentiles as an honorific title for the divine, or semi-divine, heads of the many 'Mystery' cults, with which Christianity was soon forced into open competition. Thus, so far as the Messianic titles was concerned, it was a case, if we may put it so, of the survival of the fittest.

In a number of other ways too the influence of the new circumstances is discernible. No audience outside Palestine, whatever its composition, could possibly be presumed to be as familiar with 'the things concerning Jesus' as were the first audiences in Jerusalem. It was not sufficient, therefore, to refer simply to 'Jesus of Nazareth, a man approved of God unto you by mighty works and wonders and signs which God did by him in the midst of you, even as ye yourselves know', as St. Peter had on the day of Pentecost. An audience in Antioch, or Cyprus, or Asia Minor, would not know; and the events of the life of Jesus, in particular the story of His death and Resurrection, would have to be recounted at length if the appeal of the preacher was to carry conviction. More detailed information was also necessary about the authority and significance of the Old Testament prophecies that were quoted, and about the mode of their final fulfilment. It would be asked, for instance: 'If Jesus is the divinely appointed Messiah and is now waiting in heaven "until the times of the restoration of all things", when will these "times" be, and "what will be the sign of his appearing"?' Gentile con-

---

[41] 'Christ' is, of course, the Greek translation of the Hebrew 'Messiah' = Anointed.
[42] For an example of this kind of practitioner see Acts 13.6-8. Perhaps also it is worth noting that the title 'Son of God' is found applied to Jesus, doubtless in this sense, by the Roman centurion at the Crucifixion (Matt. 27.54; Mark 15.39).
[43] In the native Aramaic the form was *maran* = 'our Lord' (cp. I Cor. 16.22).

verts especially would require to be told what precisely the relation of Jesus was, as 'Son of God' and 'Lord' to the other 'sons of god' of which they had been accustomed to speak and to the 'lords' of the Mystery cults. And further, they needed very careful instruction, not only on the theological exclusiveness of their new faith, but also on its uncompromising ethical demands; for these demands, although accepted without question by those nurtured in the traditions of Judaism, must have seemed to men brought up amid the excesses of paganism unnecessarily, even if not impossibly, exacting.

We have touched here on only a few of the more outstanding points. But enough has been said to show that, quite apart from the normal developments which might reasonably have been expected to follow in any case, the Gentile Mission raised a number of special problems which never would have been raised, and was responsible for many developments which never could have taken place, in an environment that was exclusively Jewish. The preacher to a predominantly Gentile audience was faced not only with the necessity of proclaiming the Gospel itself in far greater detail and in language that could be universally understood, but also with the task of explaining it and amplifying it in all sorts of ways to meet the peculiar needs of his interested Gentile hearers. In short, the Gentile Mission involved (to parody a modern phrase) the restatement of the Gospel in terms of Gentile thought.

And it was by a process of continual restatement that the primitive Gospel of the day of Pentecost became at last the full-blown Catholic dogmatic system. In our study of the New Testament we shall see part of this process in operation; for the individual books were written to deal with exactly the same kind of situations, and with exactly the same kind of needs, that faced the ordinary, everyday, preacher. Just as he had to restate the Gospel by word of mouth, so they restate it in more permanent form. Yet however often and in whatever form the Gospel might be restated, its essential content remained unchanged. At the centre was always Jesus —God's unique agent in His supreme act in history.

Chapter Two

ST. PAUL AND HIS
EPISTLES (I)

ALTHOUGH St. Paul was in no sense the originator of the Gentile
Mission he nevertheless soon became its most prominent figure.
His earliest missionary activities, however, were confined to Jews.
Almost immediately after his conversion, according to Acts, he
boldly entered the Damascus synagogues and 'confounded the Jews
. . . proving that this is the Christ'.[1] The result was a Jewish
plot against him, and he was forced to flee.[2] At Jerusalem it was
much the same. Like St. Stephen before him, he selected as his
particular field the Jews of the Dispersion. No doubt irritated by
his neophyte's ardour even more than by his evident ability, they
'went about to kill him'; and he was only rescued by the firmness
of his fellow-Christians, who sent him away, first to Caesarea, and
thence to his native city of Tarsus.[3]

It was in all probability during this stay in Tarsus, a city almost
entirely Gentile, that St. Paul first seriously began to consider both
the possibilities, and the claims upon him personally, of the work
that subsequently he was to make peculiarly his own. From a
reference in Galatians it might be inferred that he was aware of a
vocation to work among the Gentiles from the moment of his
conversion.[4] And such an inference is supported by the Acts
epitome of his speech before Agrippa, where a definite commission
to preach to the Gentiles is included among the words of the Risen
Jesus uttered on the Damascus road.[5] But the Acts narrative of the
conversion itself makes no mention of this commission on that
occasion;[6] and although Ananias is said to have been warned in his
vision that St. Paul was 'a chosen vessel' to bear the name of

[1] Acts 9.20,22. [2] Acts 9.23-25. [3] Acts 9.26-30.
[4] Gal. 1.16. [5] Acts 26.17,18. [6] Acts 9.4-6.

28

Jesus 'before the Gentiles and kings, and the children of Israel ',[7] he is not explicitly instructed to tell St. Paul, nor is it stated that he did so. Nor, again, in the epitome of the speech delivered in the Temple precincts at his final arrest, does St. Paul date his commission so early: on the contrary, he says that it was received later, in that very Temple, just before his departure for Tarsus.[8] In view of this conflict in the evidence, therefore, it is impossible to decide precisely when he first became conscious of his special vocation. But in Tarsus, in any event, he had ample opportunity to think things out.

How long he remained in Tarsus we do not know. But when St. Barnabas came to seek him out, took him to Antioch, and introduced him to the life of the church there,[9] his ideas in the direction of work among the Gentiles received an additional stimulus. Antioch was the fountain-head of the Gentile Mission. And it was from Antioch that St. Paul set out, together with St. Barnabas and St. Mark, to translate his ideas into action.[10]

Even so, we must resist the inevitable tendency to think of the Gentile Mission as ' a thing in itself '. Nor must we imagine that the gaining of Gentile converts was the exclusive, or indeed the primary, object of this or any other of St. Paul's journeys. As we have seen already, the Gentile Mission grew gradually and naturally out of the Jewish Mission. or all, except the most uncompromising circumcisionist, the one was the divinely ordained extension of the other; and there was nothing antagonistic between them, either in origin, or in purpose. Such, manifestly, was St. Paul's own belief. In Romans he lays down the maxim, ' To the Jew first and also to the Greek ';[11] and adherence to this maxim governed the whole of his missionary method from first to last. He preached to both Jews and Gentiles—in that order; and, wherever he found himself, he always started, if he could, with a sermon in a Jewish synagogue.

Thus, at Salamis in Cyprus, the first port of call on his first journey, he and his companions ' proclaimed the word of God in the synagogues of the Jews ',[12] although the controversy with Elymas at Paphos shows that their preaching was not limited to Jews.[13] At Antioch in Pisidia ' they went into the synagogue on the sabbath day ',[14] and St. Paul delivered a sermon of the cus-

[7] Acts 9.15. [8] Acts 22.17-21. [9] Acts 11.25,26. [10] Acts 13.1-3.
[11] Rom. 1.16; 2.9,10. [12] Acts 13.5. [13] Acts 13.6-12. [14] Acts 13.14-41.

tomary Gospel type; but on the next Sabbath the Jewish authorities, jealous of the multitudes that had assembled to hear St. Paul, became actively hostile and provoked a public disturbance, with the result that the missionaries had no choice except to direct their future efforts mainly to the conversion of Gentiles.[15]   The words ascribed to St. Paul and St. Barnabas at this moment of crisis, and addressed to the Jews, are worth quoting in full: 'It was necessary,' they declared, 'that the word of God should first be spoken to you. Seeing that ye thrust it from you, and judge yourselves unworthy of eternal life, lo, we turn to the Gentiles.   For so hath the Lord commanded us, saying, I have set thee a light of the Gentiles, that thou shouldst be for salvation unto the uttermost part of the earth.'[16]   'And as the Gentiles heard this,' the story concludes, 'they were glad, and glorified the word of God: and as many as were ordained to eternal life believed.'

A similar situation was encountered at Iconium, where 'a great multitude both of Jews and of Greeks believed'.[17]   At Lystra, the sermon delivered to the crowd of awe-struck pagans was clearly not part of the regular preaching, but an improvisation; and it was no doubt recorded as an interesting example of something out of the ordinary.[18]   At Derbe no details are given.   And although after the return to Antioch at the end of the journey the main emphasis was very naturally laid upon the success of the preaching among the Gentiles,[19] this should not be allowed to obscure the general picture. St. Paul always started with the Jews.   He was a Jew himself; and while he welcomed Gentile converts, and came to believe that God had appointed him specially as their 'apostle', he never either forgot or minimized the claims of his own nation.   As God's ancient chosen people, the Jews must always be given the first chance to hear the Gospel.   It was only where they had 'refused to hearken' that he could turn with a clear conscience to the work among the Gentiles.

As we saw in the previous chapter, St. Paul's characteristic point of view that Gentiles should be admitted to the privileges of the Gospel on exactly the same terms as Jews, and, moreover, that they were under no obligation to observe the Jewish ritual laws, gave offence, not only (as he had already discovered) to the Jews in the synagogues of the Dispersion, but also to the old-fashioned Jewish

---

[15] Acts 13.44-48.   [16] The quotation is from Isa. 49.6.   [17] Acts 14.1-6.
[18] Acts 14.8-18.   [19] Acts 14.27.

Christians at home.[20]   In the ensuing controversy, however, St.
Paul was, in effect, granted his point by the church leaders at
Jerusalem.   And he was now free to start, this time with St. Silas,
on another and more extended journey.

He began by revisiting by land, in the reverse order, the churches
of Asia Minor founded on the first journey.[21]   He then made in
a north-westerly direction to the port of Troas, and crossed into
Europe.[22]   At Philippi in Macedonia, ' a Roman colony ', there was
no synagogue; so on the Sabbath he sought out instead the Jewish
' place of prayer '.   Trouble arose through the exorcism of ' a spirit
of divination ' from a young woman named Lydia, and he and St.
Silas were thrown into prison.   As the result of a miracle the gaoler
was converted and baptized ' with all his house '.   And on the next
day the two departed at the express request of the magistrates,
leaving the gaoler, Lydia, and their households, as the nucleus of a
local church.[23]

Of the events after leaving Philippi no details are recorded until
they came to Thessalonica.   At Thessalonica there was a synagogue.
And St. Paul ' as his custom was, went in unto them, and for three
sabbath days reasoned with them from the scriptures, opening and
alleging that it behoved the Christ to suffer, and to rise again from
the dead; and that this Jesus, whom, said he, I proclaim unto you,
is the Christ '.   Some Jews were persuaded, and also many Gentiles.
But once again the jealousy of the unbelieving Jews was manifested
and the missionaries were forced to flee.[24]

At Beroea much the same thing happened.   Here, however, it
was not the Beroean Jews that caused the trouble, but Jews from
Thessalonica, who, hearing of the initial success at Beroea, ' came
thither likewise, stirring up and troubling the multitudes '.   St. Paul
was immediately sent off by sea to Athens, though St. Silas and St.
Timothy (who had joined the others at Lystra) remained behind,
having been instructed to follow at the earliest convenient opportunity.[25]

The mission of St. Paul at Athens must be pronounced his one
great failure.   In this centre of the intellectual life of the Gentile
world he was faced, as he was well aware, with an entirely different
type of audience from that to which he was accustomed.   The
Athenians were acutely conscious of their ancient philosophical

[20] See above, p. 24.   [21] Acts 15.36-16.5.   [22] Acts 16.6-11.
[23] Acts 16.12-40.   [24] Acts 17.1-9.   [25] Acts 17.10-15.

traditions, and they prided themselves on their natural curiosity and readiness to follow 'whithersoever the argument might lead'. They were in consequence only too eager to give St. Paul a hearing; while he, for his part, was only too eager to be heard. But, realizing that the normal Gospel appeal based on the evidence of the Jewish scriptures would have little effect on such an audience, he resolved on an approach through the medium of so-called 'natural' religion, and quoted freely from the pagan poets. The Athenians were not impressed. Only a mere handful 'clave unto him'. And he departed for Corinth grimly determined that he would never try such an approach again.[26]

At Corinth St. Paul found himself in a much more familiar and congenial atmosphere. He speedily made friends with a certain Aquila and his wife Priscilla, two Jews that had been expelled from Rome as a result of the edict of the Emperor Claudius, and shared lodgings with them. There was, too, a sizeable Jewish community in Corinth, and 'he reasoned in the synagogue every sabbath, and persuaded Jews and Greeks'. Soon St. Silas and St. Timothy arrived from Macedonia with a report of what had happened there since he left. But the general attitude of the Corinthian Jews proved no different from that of their brethren elsewhere. Nor did St. Paul's response. When they 'opposed themselves and blasphemed, he shook out his raiment and said unto them, Your blood be upon your own heads; I am clean: from henceforth I will go unto the Gentiles'. And the ensuing mission among the Gentiles was such a great success that St. Paul stayed on engrossed in it for eighteen months.[27]

It is to the earlier part of this stay in Corinth (more precisely, to the days immediately following the arrival of St. Silas and St. Timothy) that we must assign the writing of the first of his surviving epistles that can be dated with any certainty, namely:

I Thessalonians

The situation which called it forth is plain. At Thessalonica St. Paul had preached the normal Gospel; and many had 'turned unto God from idols, to serve a living and true God, and to wait for his

---

[26] Acts 17.16-18.1. On St. Paul's determination, see his diatribe against a philosophical presentation of the Gospel in I Cor. 1.18-2.5, which in the circumstances we can but associate with his first visit to Corinth—cp. especially I Cor. 2.1,2.
[27] Acts 18.1-11.

Son from heaven, whom he raised from the dead, even Jesus, which delivereth us from the wrath to come '.[28] The preaching had caused St. Paul himself much ' conflict '.[29] Furthermore, it had involved ' much affliction' for the converts.[30] For the unconverted Jews had not remained satisfied with merely driving St. Paul out: they had also visited their fury on the members of the infant Thessalonian church[31]—some, in all probability, had suffered martyrdom.[32] But throughout they had stood firm, and by so doing had become an example to the other churches in the district.[33] This much St. Silas and St. Timothy had reported;[34] and St. Paul accordingly joins their names with his in a written message of comfort and exhortation.

Several points are singled out for special treatment. There is, for example, the solemn warning against immorality, the perennial curse of any largely Gentile church.[35] There is also the admonition to the rank and file to respect their ecclesiastical superiors.[36] But the chief trouble seems to have arisen from the very nature of the Gospel itself.

Persecution especially had led some to fix their hopes on a speedy coming of the Day; and as the weeks went by and the Lord Jesus did not appear they became disappointed and lost their enthusiasm. St. Paul reminds them of what he had told them when he was with them, how ' the day of the Lord so cometh as a thief in the night'; and he admonishes them to ' watch and be sober' lest at the critical moment they be taken unawares.[37]

Others, apparently, had put forward the argument that if the Day was soon coming, and the present world-order was to be dissolved, it was useless to bother about this world's affairs at all: all the usual precautions against want in the future were futile. So they were giving up their customary occupations and starting out on a life of idleness, which more often than not meant becoming a burden on their fellows. St. Paul sharply recalls them to a sense of their Christian obligations, and tells them that it is their duty ' to work with their own hands' so that they may ' have need of nothing', as he had taught them himself when at Thessalonica both by word of mouth and by example.[38]

---

[28] I Thess. 1.9,10.   [29] I Thess. 2.2.   [30] I Thess 1.6.   [31] I Thess. 2.14-16.
[32] That is, if the phrase ' them that are fallen asleep in Jesus' at I Thess. 4.14 be rightly so interpreted.
[33] I Thess. 1.6-8.   [34] I Thess. 3.6.   [35] I Thess. 4.1-8.
[36] I Thess. 5.12,13.   [37] I Thess. 5.1-11.   [38] I Thess. 4.9-12; 2.9.

The question of what was to happen to the dead had also been raised. The Thessalonians had been encouraged to look forward to the appearance of Jesus and the subsequent glories of the Messianic Age. But some had died in the interval. Were they to forfeit their share in these glories? It seemed very unfair if they were—particularly so if not a few of them had been martyred in the recent persecution. Yet if they were to share, how would things be arranged? St. Paul replies that the resurrection of 'them that are fallen asleep' is a logical consequence of the resurrection of Jesus. He has the Lord's own authority for saying that those who are alive when the Day dawns (and among them, we may note, St. Paul reckons himself) will have no special privileges. In fact, 'the dead in Christ' will rise first; and then the rest, who are left alive, will be 'caught up in the clouds to meet the Lord in the air'. And in this way all will be reunited in the enjoyment of everlasting bliss. 'Wherefore,' he concludes, 'comfort one another with these words.'[39]

Thus, the Epistle provides an interesting illustration of at any rate one of the ways in which the primitive Gospel grew. To begin with, the Gospel alone was everywhere sufficient to meet the needs of its hearers. But situations soon arose in every church in which clarification and amplification were essential if unfortunate and harmful misconceptions were to be avoided. And St. Paul, in writing to Thessalonica, had primarily this in mind.

Towards the end of his eighteen months stay in Corinth St. Paul was charged by the Jews in the public courts with 'persuading men to worship God contrary to the Law'. The Roman proconsul, Gallio, saw immediately that by 'the Law' only the Jewish Law was meant, and the case collapsed.[40] Soon afterwards St. Paul decided to return to Antioch, and, together with Aquila and Priscilla, took ship for Ephesus. At Ephesus, although his visit was to be only temporary, he 'entered into the synagogue and reasoned with the Jews', who were surprisingly friendly and urged him to stay longer. But he refused. And leaving Aquila and Priscilla behind him with a promise to return, he sailed for Palestine, landed at Caesarea, and from there 'went down to Antioch'.[41]

Having spent what Acts rather vaguely describes as 'some time' at Antioch, he set out once more on his travels. Just at the begin-

[39] I Thess. 4.13-18.   [40] Acts 18.12-17.   [41] Acts 18.18-22.

ning of his second journey he had revisited by land the churches of Derbe, Lystra, Iconium, and Pisidian Antioch, founded on the first journey, so now, at the beginning of the third, he 'went through the region of Galatia and Phrygia in order establishing all the disciples'.[42] But this accomplished, instead of turning north-west to Troas, as he had before, he went on due west to Ephesus to fulfil his promise and resume his preaching.[43]

Since his departure a flourishing little church had been founded there by Aquila and Priscilla. In particular a learned Jew from Alexandria named Apollos had been converted; and he, after preach-ing at Ephesus with some effect, had crossed over to continue his labours in Corinth.[44] Strange to relate, the Ephesian Jews still remained friendly, so that for three months after his arrival St. Paul was allowed to preach in the synagogue without opposition. But then—the inevitable. When some Jews showed themselves 'hardened and disobedient' and maligned the Christians openly, St. Paul moved his headquarters elsewhere and conducted what seems to have been the most vigorously pursued and the most widely successful of all his missions from the school of a certain Tyrannus. Not only was his preaching accompanied by miracles which im-pressed the Ephesian populace enormously, but also the city was made the base for more extended operations in the neighbourhood, so that 'all they which dwelt in Asia [i.e. the Roman province of which Ephesus was the capital] heard the word of the Lord, both Jews and Greeks'.[45]

When this had continued for the space of two years, St. Paul, always anxious to go further afield, decided on a journey to Rome. He laid his plans carefully. First, he would visit again the churches of Macedonia and Greece, founded on the second journey: next he would go to Jerusalem—primarily, it appears, to present in person to the impoverished mother-church a monetary offering which he had been at pains for some time to collect from her dutiful daughters, the Gentile churches; and then, so he thought, he would start for the capital of the world. Accordingly, he sent St. Timothy and a colleague into Macedonia in advance, while he himself made his final preparations at leisure.[46]

His last days in Ephesus, however, were disturbed by an unfor-tunate anti-Christian riot. Into the details of this riot there is no

[42] Acts 18.23.   [43] Acts 19.1.   [44] Acts 18.24-28.
[45] Acts 19.8-20.   [46] Acts 19.21,22.

need to enter, since St. Paul's plans were in no way upset. 'After the uproar was ceased,' the Acts narrative states, 'Paul having sent for the disciples and exhorted them, took leave of them, and departed for to go into Macedonia. And when he had gone through those parts, and had given them much exhortation, he came into Greece.'[47]

It was during the last few months of the two years in Ephesus, and during the journey through Macedonia, that the epistles to Corinth were written.

I and II Corinthians

The First Epistle clearly belongs to the period after St. Paul had despatched St. Timothy and his colleague into Macedonia, but before he himself left Ephesus—i.e. it fits exactly into the situation described in Acts 19.21,22. St. Paul says in the Epistle that he is remaining for the moment at Ephesus,[48] but that he intends to come to Corinth shortly when he has 'passed through Macedonia'.[49] Meanwhile, he has sent St. Timothy on in front, and he asks the Corinthians to give him a warm welcome, if, as seems probable, he arrives first.[50]

The reasons for writing are also clear. All was not well at Corinth. A group of Christians who had recently come over to Ephesus by sea ('they which are of the household of Chloe') had told St. Paul that the Corinthian church was split by factions, each purporting to follow a different leader. Some were 'of Paul': others 'of Apollos': others 'of Cephas' (i.e. St. Peter, who would thus seem to have visited Corinth); while yet others preened themselves on being 'of Christ'—and therefore, presumably, absolved from acknowledging any human leadership at all.[51]

After exhorting them all to 'speak the same thing' and to drop their party bickerings, St. Paul proceeds to explain carefully what he conceives to be the true relationship between himself, his apparent rivals, and the ordinary Christian, in the building up of the Church as a whole. The progress of the Church Universal, he tells the Corinthians, is ten thousand times more important than the success of any merely local party; and loyalty to Christ stands in a completely different category from the perfectly natural loyalty which an individual might feel towards a particular Christian leader.

---

[47] Acts 19.23–20.2.   [48] I Cor. 16.8.   [49] I Cor. 16.5; see also 4.19 and 11.34.
[50] I Cor. 4.17; 16.10.   [51] I Cor. 1.11,12.

Even so, these human leaders, or 'ministers' as he calls them, are necessary and have their functions to fulfil: they have the task of planting the seed of the Gospel in the first instance, and later on of watering it and tending it until by the power of God the struggling plant reaches maturity—a state, which, St. Paul rather pointedly reminds his readers, is still for them a very long way off. He himself, Apollos, and St. Peter, are all equally 'ministers of Christ and stewards of the mysteries of God': all three are fellow-labourers in the same great work; and together they share the same divine commission. True, their functions are not identical. Each has his specially allotted task. But this makes no difference to their status as 'ministers'. The only difference it might make, and in St. Paul's view obviously does make, is a difference in authority over the affairs of particular churches. He was himself the founder of the church at Corinth, and for that reason he claims a special authority over its members, as a father over his 'beloved children'. And he intends to use that authority to 'admonish' them. 'What will ye?' he bluntly asks, 'shall I come to you with a rod, or in love and a spirit of meekness?'[52]

The same tone of fatherly admonition pervades the rest of the Epistle. St. Paul is concerned about what he has heard. A gross case of incest has been reported.[53] There is widespread and often open immorality.[54] The Corinthians have also developed a habit of dragging their many quarrels before the heathen law-courts.[55] For all these failings they both merit and receive severe rebukes.

Then, at the beginning of chapter 7, the form of the Epistle changes. A number of questions are dealt with successively, and each is introduced by the formula 'Now concerning . . .' First come marriage, divorce, and sexual relations.[56] Next, the treatment of virgins.[57] Then, 'things sacrificed to idols'—a difficult question about whether or not a Christian might eat meat that had been offered as a sacrifice in a pagan temple and later sold in the public shops.[58] Then, 'spiritual gifts'—which of them was the best to have?[59] And finally, details about the collection, which, as we have seen, St. Paul had been planning for some time to take as a gift from the Gentile churches to the mother-church at Jerusalem.[60]

[52] I Cor. 1.10-4.21.
[55] I Cor. 6.1-11.
[58] I Cor. 8.1-11.1.
[53] I Cor. 5.1-8.
[56] I Cor. 7.1-24.
[59] I Cor. 12.1-14.40.
[54] I Cor. 5.9-13; 6.12-20.
[57] I Cor. 7.25-40.
[60] I Cor. 16.1-4.

Other matters also come up. Thus, the proper conduct of Christian worship is treated as a sort of appendix to the teaching on 'things sacrificed to idols';[61] and the perplexities of the Corinthians about the resurrection are dealt with fully in chapter 15. Throughout we can see that St. Paul is anxious, not only to guard his 'children' from error, but also to lead them on to a finer appreciation of the true nature and obligations of their Christian profession.

But before we leave the First Epistle one additional point is worth attention because it illustrates the close contact which was maintained between St. Paul and his churches. The words at the beginning of chapter 7 ('Now concerning the things whereof ye wrote') imply that the Corinthians had written a letter which St. Paul is answering. Who brought it we do not know. It may have been brought by one of the many traders who journeyed between Corinth and Ephesus in the normal course of business: possibly it was brought by 'them which are of the household of Chloe'; but more probably by Stephanas, Fortunatus, and Achaicus, who are mentioned as having recently arrived in Ephesus at 16.17. There St. Paul says that he rejoices at their coming 'for that which was lacking on your part they supplied', which seems to mean that they filled out by word of mouth the contents of a letter. If this be so, St. Paul will have started writing on the report of 'those of Chloe'. Half-way through Stephanas, Fortunatus, and Achaicus, will have arrived with a letter from the Corinthians asking a series of questions. So St. Paul concludes with direct answers to these questions, supplementing wherever necessary on the basis of what the three bearers of the letter had told him. And dare we conjecture further that it was the same three who took the First Epistle with them on their return to Corinth?

The circumstances in which the Second Epistle was written are more obscure. From several references it might appear at first sight to belong to the period immediately after St. Paul had left Ephesus and was journeying through Macedonia.[62] But there are two serious obstacles in the way of accepting this solution as entirely satisfactory.

In the first place, in two passages towards the end of the Epistle St. Paul says that he is about to come to Corinth for 'the third time'.[63] According to Acts, however, he only visited Corinth

[61] I Cor. 11.2-34.   [62] II Cor. 1.16; 2.12,13; 7.5; 8.1; 9.2.   [63] II Cor. 12.14; 13.1.

twice altogether—once on his second journey when he founded the church there, and again on his third journey after he had 'gone through Macedonia'.[64] Moreover, near the beginning of the Epistle he affirms that he had determined 'that I would not come again to you with sorrow';[65] and the context makes it only too plain that the visit he is referring to was a painful recollection for all concerned. He cannot, therefore, be referring to his first visit. Nor is it likely that he is referring to the second of the visits mentioned in Acts, for if so we shall have to suppose that his declared intention to come 'the *third* time' (and he speaks as if he was almost about to arrive in Corinth) was never carried out. Far more probable is it that Acts has passed over what was in reality the second visit, and that what now appears in Acts as the second was in fact the third. In that case, shortly before his departure from Ephesus, St. Paul will have hurried across by sea to reprimand the Corinthians in person—i.e. he will have carried out the threat of the First Epistle to 'come unto them with a rod'.[66] We may assume that such a visit would be painful; while the circumstances and the apparent lack of results, combined with the incidental nature of the visit and the fact that it was only of brief duration, will sufficiently account for its omission from the narrative of Acts.

The other obstacle in the way of accepting the easy solution of the dating of the Second Epistle is that St. Paul refers twice in it to a letter he had written 'out of much affliction and anguish of heart', which had 'made' the Corinthians 'sorry'.[67] It is hardly likely that these references are to the First Epistle, which, although severe in parts, is on the whole comparatively mild, and gives no indication whatever that it was written in 'affliction and anguish of heart'. There is, of course, the possibility that St. Paul is referring to a letter written after the First Epistle, which the Corinthians conveniently lost! But again it is far more probable, as is generally held to-day, that the references are indeed to a letter written after the First Epistle, but that that letter, so far from being lost, has been preserved, although doubtless not in its entirety, in the last four chapters of our present Second Epistle.

No one who reads the Second Epistle through can fail to be struck by the marked change of tone at the beginning of chapter 10. The previous nine chapters breathe an atmosphere of thankfulness

---

[64] Acts 18.1-18; 20.2,3.   [65] II Cor. 2.1.   [66] I Cor. 4.21.   [67] II Cor. 2.4; 7.8.

and relief;[68] but now St. Paul starts to argue, to defend himself, and to threaten.[69]   His description of the letter which made the Corinthians 'sorry' agrees very well with the contents of the last four chapters; and there are several apparent cross-references, which give the impression that in chapters 1-9 he is harking back to what he had already written in chapters 10-13.[70]   If we add to this the observation that all the passages which are used to date the Second Epistle occur in chapters 1-9, we are led to the conclusion that it was these nine chapters only which were written from Macedonia before St. Paul's last visit to Corinth; and that chapters 10-13 are part of another letter, written after the First Epistle but before II Cor. 1-9, which have been tacked on at the end by a zealous editor who rescued them from the oblivion to which many of the Corinthians were no doubt only too willing to consign them.

Thus, the Second Epistle introduces us to the later stages of a quarrel between St. Paul and the Corinthian church.   It has appeared already from the First Epistle that the relations between them, even then, were not entirely harmonious, and that St. Paul, as the Corinthians' spiritual father, had no hesitation in administering some sharp rebukes.   These rebukes, it seems, had little effect and only served to widen the breach.   In consequence, St. Paul not only visited Corinth again in person, but also followed up his visit by writing a much sterner letter (II Cor. 10-13) in order to recall the Corinthians to a better frame of mind.   This apparently had the desired effect and the matter was finally settled by the writing from Macedonia of II Cor. 1-9.

The trouble manifestly centred on St. Paul's claim to authority. It is plain from the First Epistle that there were a number at Corinth who disputed that authority; and from the defence that St. Paul puts forward in II Cor. 10-13 it is possible to infer at any rate something of the grounds on which they disputed it.   Compared with other well-known figures, his opponents maintained, St. Paul was demonstrably inferior.   He was deficient alike in personality and in powers of speech:[71] he had been granted no 'visions' or 'revelations':[72] he wrought no miracles or 'mighty works':[73] he was, indeed, completely devoid of all the so-called 'spiritual gifts'.[74] It was doubtful, therefore, whether he could rightly be regarded as

[68] e.g. II Cor. 7.4-7; 9.15.   [69] e.g. II Cor. 10.1ff.; 13.2.
[70] Cp. e.g. II Cor. 1.23 with 13.2; 2.3 with 13.10; 2.9 with 10.6.
[71] II Cor. 10.10; cp. 10.1 and 11.16.
[72] II Cor. 12.1.   [73] II Cor. 12.12.   [74] II Cor. 10.2.

either a true 'apostle'[73] or a genuine 'minister of Christ'.[75] And
for such a man to claim paramount authority over a church so distinguished for its gifts of the Spirit as the Corinthian was as
ridiculous as it was impertinent.

St. Paul counters these charges with vigour. His meekness is
not to be confused with feebleness: he is deliberately following in
the footsteps of the Lord.[76] His deficiencies in 'spiritual gifts'
are rather apparent than real: he can produce evidence of visions,
revelations, and miracles, which will prove that he is 'in nothing
behind the very chiefest apostles' if anyone cares to examine it.[77]
But any semblance of 'glorying' through a recital of the evidence
is distasteful to him; for all these things are in his view of relatively
minor importance. 'I reckon,' he repeats, 'that I am not a whit
behind the very chiefest apostles.'[78] And he rests his case on his
own life history as a Christian preacher, with its manifold labours,
dangers, and persecutions, all patiently and cheerfully borne with
no motive of personal gain, but simply and solely that as many as
possible (and among these he specially singles out the Corinthians)
might receive 'the gospel of God for nought'.[79] There, in the
record of his sufferings, is ample proof of the genuineness of his
apostleship. And he concludes by repeating his claim and by gently
reminding his readers that he is prepared to maintain it to the bitter
end. 'I write these things,' he says, 'while absent, that I may not
when present deal sharply, according to the authority which the
Lord gave me for building up, and not for casting down.'[80]

The letter containing this defence seems to have been written just
before St. Paul left Ephesus on his way into Macedonia, and to
have been sent to Corinth by Titus, who was instructed to bring
St. Paul a report of its reception as soon as possible. At Troas St.
Paul paused, full of anxiety and apprehension: but no Titus
appeared.[81] So he went on into Macedonia more worried than
ever.[82] Here at last Titus found him and was able to tell him that
all was well. The Corinthian church as a body had publicly dis-
sociated itself from the attitude of his opponents and had taken
disciplinary measures against them: the genuineness of his apostleship was now unquestioned and his claim to authority conceded;
and, what was more, the Corinthians were all longing to see him

[73] II Cor. 12.12.   [75] II Cor. 11.23.   [76] II Cor. 10.1.
[77] II Cor. 12.1-13.   [78] II Cor. 11.5.   [79] II Cor. 11.1-33.
[80] II Cor. 13.10.   [81] II Cor. 2.12,13.   [82] II Cor. 2.13; 7.5.

to express their sorrow personally and convince him of their change of heart.[83]

In these circumstances St. Paul sits down and pens to Corinth an immediate expression of his relief. The God whom he blesses in his opening paragraph is 'the Father of mercies and God of all comfort'[84]: his own 'mouth is open' to the Corinthians, his 'heart is enlarged'[85]: he is 'filled with comfort' and 'overflowing with joy'[86]: 'thanks be to God', he cries, 'for his unspeakable gift'.[87] He adds some further remarks about the progress of the collection, stressing the enthusiasm with which the Macedonian churches are contributing, and hoping that this may serve as a spur to the efforts of the Corinthians.[88] And the letter is sent off at once by Titus and two companions.[89]

From the above reconstruction it follows that St. Paul wrote not two, but three, letters to Corinth. A passage in the First Epistle, however, makes it certain that we must reckon with yet a fourth. When dealing there with the immoralities prevalent at Corinth St. Paul says distinctly: 'I wrote unto you in my epistle to have no company with fornicators';[90] and he goes on to explain what he meant in the letter referred to. Clearly, then, what we now know as the First Epistle was not in fact the first, but was preceded by an earlier or 'previous' letter (as it is commonly called).

In all probability this letter has been lost. Many scholars, though, believe that a fragment of it survives in II Cor. 6.14-7.1. Not only do these verses seriously disturb the flow of the section in which they occur (6.11-7.4, dealing with the 'open-hearted' relationship now re-established between St. Paul and the Corinthians), but also their contents enjoining separation from 'unbelievers' and 'all defilement of flesh and spirit' tally closely with the injunction 'to have no company with fornicators'. It is in consequence suggested that an odd leaf of St. Paul's earliest letter of warning against immoralities has accidentally been interpolated between two leaves of his final letter of reconciliation. Whether this be so or not it is impossible to say. But of one thing we may be sure—that there was a 'previous' letter. It accordingly seems likely that St. Paul wrote in all *four* letters to Corinth, of which only one (the First Epistle) survives to-day intact.

---

[83] II Cor. 7.6-16.   [84] II Cor. 1.3,4.   [85] II Cor. 6.11.
[86] II Cor. 7.4.   [87] II Cor. 9.15.   [88] II Cor. 8.1ff.; 9.1ff.
[89] II Cor. 8.16-24.   [90] I Cor. 5.9.

The sequence of events which the correspondence discloses may now be summarized as follows:

(1) Some time during his stay at Ephesus on his third journey, probably towards the end of it, St. Paul hears about the state of affairs at Corinth and writes a letter warning the Corinthians against immorality and associations with immoral persons—i.e. the ' previous letter '.

(2) ' Those of Chloe ' arrive at Ephesus with a report that the Corinthian church is divided and that St. Paul's position and authority are being openly challenged. They are soon followed by Stephanas, Fortunatus, and Achaicus, who not only bring a letter from the Corinthians asking certain definite questions, but also confirm by word of mouth St. Paul's own impression that the situation is deteriorating. He accordingly writes another letter, kindly but firm, answering the Corinthians' questions and admonishing them on a number of other points on which he thinks admonition necessary—i.e. our I Corinthians.

(3) St. Paul hears, perhaps from St. Timothy, who has returned to Ephesus, that what he has written has had no effect and that the situation is worse than ever. He decides hurriedly to visit Corinth himself. But he is rebuffed and comes back bitterly disappointed.

(4) He therefore writes another, much stronger, letter ' out of much affliction and anguish of heart ', and sends it to Corinth by Titus—i.e. the letter preserved in part in II Cor. 10-13.

(5) Soon afterwards he leaves Ephesus by way of Troas to carry through his projected tour of the churches of Macedonia ' afflicted on every side '.

(6) In Macedonia Titus finds him with the welcome news that his wildest dreams have been realized: his opponents have been worsted: the Corinthians have at last seen the error of their ways; and they long to assure him in person of the reality of their change of heart.

(7) St. Paul immediately sends back by Titus and his two companions a written expression of his relief and his hopes for the future—i.e. II Cor. 1-9.

And then, his work in Macedonia completed, he himself ' came into Greece '.[91]

It is not stated in Acts in so many words that the ' three months '[92]

---

[91] Acts 20.2.   [92] Acts 20.3.

during which St. Paul remained in 'Greece' were spent at Corinth. But in view of the two facts that Corinth was the provincial capital and that we know from the Corinthian Epistles that St. Paul had very special reasons for visiting it just then, there can be little doubt that Corinth was his main objective even if he did not remain there the whole three months. In any event, it is to these three months, and to Corinth or its immediate neighbourhod, that we must assign the despatch, and probably also the writing, of the longest and most systematic of all St. Paul's epistles, viz.:

Romans

The indications which converge to establish this dating are: (i) the bearer of the Epistle was Phoebe, 'a servant of the church that is at Cenchreae',[93] and Cenchreae was the port of Corinth; (ii) at the time the Epistle was despatched St. Paul was staying with a certain 'Gaius',[94] who is most naturally identified with the Gaius mentioned in I Corinthians as one of the few converts at Corinth that St. Paul baptized himself;[95] and (iii) St. Paul's words in the Epistle, 'But now, I say, I go unto Jerusalem, ministering unto the saints. For it hath been the good pleasure of Macedonia and Achaia to make a certain contribution for the poor among the saints that are at Jerusalem,'[96] fit exactly the situation after he had 'gone through' Macedonia and come into 'Greece' [= Achaia] and before he left for Jerusalem with the collection, of which we hear both in his letters to Corinth[97] and later on in Acts.[98]

For some time it had been St. Paul's intention to visit Rome, but a number of things had happened to prevent him. Now, his tour of Macedonia and Achaia completed, and the offerings of the Gentile churches ready for presentation, his labours 'in these regions' are at an end. After the presentation at Jerusalem he will be free to journey to the West. So he writes to prepare the Romans for his coming. He hopes that they will be ready to receive him and that he may accomplish some useful work among them; and also that they will assist him in a further project—the planting of the Gospel in the as yet virgin soil of Spain.[99]

St. Paul, of course, had not founded the church at Rome. He had never previously been there; and he was personally unknown

---

[93] Rom. 16.1.   [94] Rom. 16.23.   [95] I Cor. 1.14.   [96] Rom. 15.25,26.
[97] I Cor. 16.1ff.; II Cor. 8.1ff.; 9.1ff.   [98] Acts 24.17.
[99] Rom. 1.11-15; 15.15-29; cp. Acts 19.21.

to the great majority of Roman Christians. He had, moreover, the strongest possible aversion from ever seeming to 'build upon another man's foundation'.[100] Consequently, he was not able to instruct the Romans on any particular points of doctrine or ethics as he had instructed the Thessalonians and the Corinthians, for he had no inside knowledge of what the particular points were on which the Romans needed instruction. Nor could he presume to write to them as a 'father', since to do so would have meant claiming an authority over the church at Rome, which in other circumstances he knew well enough he would have been the first to repudiate. So he was forced to choose as the main theme of his letter a more general topic.

The evidence of the Epistle makes it clear that, as was the case with the churches St. Paul himself had founded, the Roman Christians were of mixed origin, some Jews,[101] some Gentiles.[102] And it was this fact that probably first suggested to St. Paul the suitability of sending them a full and reasoned account of his own teaching about God's dealings in the past with both Jews and Gentiles, and their present relationship to one another in the Universal Church of Christ.

Yet there was doubtless also a more personal reason which led St. Paul to select this topic. The admission to full church membership of the earliest Gentile converts had been the signal for the most violent controversy; and, although the decision reached at Jerusalem had been in favour of admitting Gentiles to membership on exactly the same terms as Jews,[103] there were still many old-fashioned Jewish Christians who refused to accept it, and who persisted in maintaining that the Gentile Mission was an illegitimate development and a violation of true Christian principles. St. Paul, as its leading protagonist, was naturally in their eyes particularly obnoxious, and they soon came to look upon him as the arch-enemy of the faith. Their favourite method of attack seems to have been to visit the churches that he founded and attempt to set his 'children' against him by denying both his credentials as an apostle and the validity of the Gospel which he preached, setting forth at the same time what they represented as the genuine Gospel in all its fullness, emphasizing the obligation of all Christians, whatever their origin, to observe strictly the Mosaic Law, and stressing

[100] Rom. 15.20.
[102] e.g. Rom. 1.13; 11.13.
[101] e.g. Rom. 4.1; 7.1-6.
[103] See above, pp. 24, 25.

especially the need for Gentile converts to submit to the rite of circumcision. There are manifest traces of such anti-Pauline circumcisionist activity in the churches of Galatia,[104] and in other churches as well.[105] From a passage in II Corinthians ('Are they Hebrews? so am I. Are they Israelites? so am I. Are they the seed of Abraham? so am I.')[106] it is probable that much of the opposition to St. Paul at Corinth proceeded from the same source. And circumcisionists too may have been active at Rome. At any rate St. Paul was uneasy. The Romans had never seen him. They had merely heard about him. They knew that he was the centre of controversy and that there were many who were violently opposed to him. He was eager that they should welcome him, but anxious lest any malicious rumours should have predisposed them against him. So in order to forestall any coldness engendered by misunderstanding, he characteristically resolved to defend himself in advance by putting the Romans in possession of his case some time before his arrival.

That is why the Epistle inevitably seems to the reader to be more of a theological treatise than a letter. St. Paul is concerned to state his position on an issue of fundamental importance. 'I am not ashamed of the gospel,' he writes after the introductory verses, 'for it is the power of God unto salvation to every one that believeth; to the Jew first, and also to the Greek. For therein is revealed a righteousness of God by faith unto faith: as it is written, But the righteous shall live by faith.'[107] And in this declaration, with its unqualified assertion that through the preaching of the Gospel salvation is now offered to Gentile no less than to Jew, and its emphasis on faith as the essential pre-condition of that salvation for both Jew and Gentile alike, he strikes the keynote of the Epistle.

In times past, he argues, God revealed Himself to the Gentiles through Nature and to the Jews through the Law. The possession of the Law, of course, meant that the Jews were especially privileged; but it did not mean, as some of them all too readily assumed, either that they were superior to the Gentiles as a race, or that as individuals they necessarily stood closer to God. God required that all men should respond to His revelation: He demanded righteousness from Jews and Gentiles equally; and His judgement was strictly impartial. A righteous Gentile was in His sight more

[104] See below, p. 58.   [105] Cp. e.g. Phil. 3.2ff.   [106] II Cor. 11.22.
[107] Rom. 1.16,17.

acceptable than an unrighteous Jew; for 'with God' there was 'no respect of persons'.[108]

In practice, however, the standard of righteousness demanded by God had rarely, if ever, been attained. Both Jews and Gentiles are all 'under sin'[109] and have 'fallen short of the glory of God'.[110] The old way to righteousness, which was based on 'works', is in consequence demonstrably bankrupt.[111] In the Gospel a new way has been substituted; for the Gospel speaks of a 'righteousness of God through faith in Jesus Christ' which is available to all that believe without 'distinction',[112] whether Jews by birth or Gentiles, whether circumcised or not.[113]

Yet this new way is by no means so novel as many might suppose. It was 'witnessed by the law and the prophets'.[114] It was also plainly foreshadowed by the specific case of Abraham. 'Abraham believed God,' we are told in Genesis, 'and it was reckoned unto him for righteousness.' Not, therefore, because of his 'works' was Abraham accounted 'righteous'. Nor yet was it because he was circumcised; for the words 'it was reckoned unto him for righteousness' occur in Gen. 15.6, and the institution of circumcision is not recorded until two chapters later. The conclusion follows that in the 'reckoning' of Abraham's 'righteousness' his 'faith' was not only primary, but also the sole determining factor. His 'works' were of no significance, while circumcision was merely the 'seal' of a 'righteousness' already 'reckoned'. And through his dealings of old with Abraham God shows His eternal purpose for the whole of the human race. That purpose was finally and fully revealed through the death and resurrection of Jesus, and is now declared in the Christian Gospel. For the words 'it was reckoned unto him for righteousness' were not written for Abraham's sake alone, but for the sake of faithful Christians also, 'unto whom it shall be reckoned, who believe on him that raised Jesus our Lord from the dead, who was delivered up for our trespasses, and was raised for our justification'.[115]

Thus, neither 'works' nor circumcision are the appointed ways to 'righteousness'; 'faith' alone is what God requires.[116] And as many years before, when asked by the terrified gaoler at Philippi 'What must I do to be saved?' St. Paul had replied in the simplest

[108] Rom. 1.18-3.8.   [109] Rom. 3.9.   [110] Rom. 3.23.
[111] Rom. 3.20.   [112] Rom. 3.22.   [113] Rom. 3.29,30.
[114] Rom. 3.21.   [115] Rom. 4.1-25.   [116] Rom. 5.1.

terms 'Believe on the Lord Jesus and thou shalt be saved,'[117] so now he maintains, though in a more complicated theological argument, the same unique necessity of a 'faith' whose focal point is Jesus. The great act of 'reconciliation' between God and man was accomplished once for all upon the cross.[118] Yet it still remains for each individual to claim his share in God's 'free gift'.[119] This can only be done by 'faith'. And the 'faith' of which St. Paul writes is not mere credence, the acceptance of the truth of certain intellectual propositions, but the complete and personal trust of the believer in his Lord. The 'seal' of that 'faith' is no longer circumcision but baptism, whereby a mystical relationship is established between Christ and the believer. Just as Christ Himself died upon the cross, so the Christian, by his confession of faith before baptism, 'dies' mystically 'to sin'. Just as Christ Himself was taken down from the cross and buried in the tomb, so the Christian is buried in the baptismal waters[120] to everything that has gone before. And just as Christ 'was raised from the dead through the glory of the Father', so too the Christian, when he comes up from the water, is raised to 'newness of life' in Him.[121]

The result is a new sense of freedom and a God-given power of achievement, of which the 'end' is 'eternal life'.[122] Since the Law and its ordinances belong to the past,[123] there can be no verdict of 'condemnation' for 'them that are in Christ Jesus'.[124] As baptized believers they now live 'in Christ' entirely; and in proportion as they submit themselves to the promptings and guidance of the Spirit which dwells within them, they both manifest the reality of their Christian status as adopted 'sons of God', and claim their rightful inheritance as 'joint-heirs with Christ'.[125] For those thus mystically united with the victory of their Risen Lord the failure, frustrations, and agonies, of life in this present world are robbed of their normal terrors: Christ Himself suffered, endured, and conquered; and His victory is the pledge of ours.[126] 'Who shall separate us from the love of Christ? Shall tribulation, or anguish, or persecution, or famine, or nakedness, or peril, or sword? . . . Nay, in all these things we are more than conquerors through him that loved us. For I am persuaded, that neither death,

---

[117] Acts 16.31.   [118] Rom. 5. 6-11.   [119] Rom. 5.12-21.
[120] Baptism in the early Church was in all probability by total immersion and not by sprinkling.
[121] Rom. 6.1-11.   [122] Rom. 6.12-23.   [123] Rom. 7.1-6.
[124] Rom. 8.1.   [125] Rom. 8.2-17.   [126] Rom. 8.18-34.

nor life, nor angels, nor principalities, nor things present, nor things to come, nor powers, nor height, nor depth, nor any other creature, shall be able to separate us from the love of God, which is in Christ Jesus our Lord.'[127]

After this outburst of triumphant assurance St. Paul comes immediately down to earth. Experience had shown that while in theory the Gospel might be preached without distinction ' to the Jew first and also to the Greek ', in practice it was the Greek for the most part who responded whereas the Jew did not. This rejection of the Gospel by the Jews raised for St. Paul a serious problem, especially as he was, of course, by origin a Jew himself. He and his co-religionists had always been brought up to regard themselves as God's chosen people. But if the Gospel, and not the Law, was now the appointed means of salvation, and if, in addition, the Jews were now almost entirely outside its orbit, must it not be admitted that God, so to speak, had changed His mind, that He had repudiated His initial choice, and that His ' word ' had ' come to nought '?[128]

St. Paul's answer takes the form of a fundamental re-examination and re-interpretation of the traditional doctrine of divine election. He lays it down to start with that ' they are not all Israel, that are of Israel: neither because they are of Abraham's seed are they all children '—i.e. membership of the elect community is in no way guaranteed by mere physical descent from Abraham : rather is it the result in each instance of a direct choice on the part of God. And he goes on to prove this assertion from the Old Testament. Thus, it is clear from the evidence of Genesis that of all the sons of Abraham only Isaac was the ' child of promise ': similarly, of the two sons of Isaac, Jacob was preferred to Esau. The true ' children of God ' are therefore chosen by a process of repeated selection; and the words of Malachi ' Jacob I loved, but Esau I hated ' are in consequence to be given a far wider application than they would seem to have in their immediate context, since they are in fact a succinct and pregnant description of God's mode of operation in each successive generation.[129]

Some might criticize God's choice as arbitrary. To this objection St. Paul replies that just as the potter has absolute control over his clay, so God the Creator has absolute control over His creation : He is an inalienable right to ' make known the riches of his glory

---

[127] Rom. 8.35-39.   [128] Rom. 9.1-6.   [129] Rom. 9.6-13.

D

upon vessels of mercy' when and where He wills. If He now exercises that right by selecting His 'vessels of mercy' without distinction, 'not from the Jews only but also from the Gentiles', there can be no reasonable ground for complaint. The Gentiles, in so far as they have responded to the Gospel, have demonstrated beyond dispute that they have 'attained to righteousness, even the righteousness which is of faith': the Jews, in so far as they have rejected the Gospel, have demonstrated that they have not attained. Furthermore, this situation was foreseen long ago by the prophets who spoke of the 'disobedience' of Israel, of the salvation of a 'remnant' only, and of God's call of a 'people which was not my people'. It cannot be argued, therefore, that God has changed His mind.[130]

Yet St. Paul, as an 'Israelite of the stock of Abraham', will not admit the permanence of such a situation. It is a stage, and no more than a stage, in the working out of God's plan of universal salvation. As the olive-grower drastically prunes his trees and grafts wild branches into the cultivated stems,[131] so God has 'broken off' the seemingly luxuriant branches of the parent Jewish stock and is grafting in 'wild' Gentile branches, in order that both may grow together and produce more abundant fruit. The 'hardening in part' which has befallen Israel is, therefore, not accidental. God has not 'cast off' His people for ever. His apparent rejection of them is but part of His far-reaching design to save all His creatures. Soon the evident salvation of so many Gentiles will begin to 'provoke' the Jews 'to jealousy' in the sense that their unbelief will yield to faith; and, when 'the fulness of the Gentiles be come in', then 'all Israel shall be saved', and God's plan will be at last complete. 'For as ye [i.e. the Gentiles] in time past were disobedient to God, but now have obtained mercy by their [i.e. the Jews'] disobedience, even so have these also now been disobedient, that by the mercy shown to you they also may now obtain mercy. For God hath shut up all unto disobedience, that he might have mercy upon all.'[132]

From this elaborate doctrinal statement St. Paul passes to other, less controversial, matters. The Romans must remember that the

[130] Rom. 9.14-10.21.
[131] It is to be noted that St. Paul has got his metaphor the wrong way round. One obtains the best results by grafting cultivated slips into wild stems, and not *vice versa*!
[132] Rom. 11.1-32.

profession of Christianity involves certain clearly defined practical consequences. They are to offer themselves continually as 'a living sacrifice, holy, acceptable to God' : [133] as subjects of the Empire they must recognize that 'the powers that be are ordained of God' and submit themselves without complaint to the duly constituted temporal authorities: [134] as members of the Church they must realize their obligations as individuals to contribute to the corporate life of the 'one body in Christ'[135]; and by a proper regard for the rights and needs of others they must demonstrate 'in the sight of all men' the working of the Christian law of love.[136] Indeed, by the practice of a universal tolerance alone, a tolerance in which Jew and Gentile are joined in one, can they prove the reality of their faith.[137] The need is urgent. 'For now is our salvation nearer to us than when we first believed. The night is far spent, and the day is at hand : let us therefore cast off the works of darkness, and let us put on the armour of light.'[138]

The Epistle concludes with some remarks about St. Paul's personal affairs,[139] followed by a long list of salutations and a final doxology.[140] We may note here especially 16.22—'I Tertius, who wrote the epistle, salute you in the Lord.' From this verse and from others elsewhere[141] it appears that it was St. Paul's practice to dictate his letters to a secretary, and then, if he felt so inclined, to add a few words at the end in his own hand, much as a modern business man will occasionally add a hand-written postscript to a type-written letter that has been brought to him for signature. In this instance there is no indication whether St. Paul added anything himself or not; but, on the other hand, it is the only instance in which the name of one of his secretaries has been preserved. The verse is a private message of greeting to his own friends, slipped in near the end, by the otherwise unknown Tertius.

In one manuscript of the Epistle the words 'in Rome' at 1.7 and 'those that are in Rome' at 1.15 are lacking; and this general form of address ('to all that are beloved of God, called to be saints' with no mention of Rome) was certainly known to more than one early commentator. There are, too, significant differences between the manuscripts in the placing of the final doxology: the majority place it where to-day we are accustomed to read it—at the end

[133] Rom. 12.1,2. [134] Rom. 13.1-7. [135] Rom. 12.3-8.
[136] Rom. 12.9-21; 13.8-10. [137] Rom. 14.1-15.13. [138] Rom. 13.11-14.
[139] Rom. 15.14-33. [140] Rom. 16.1-27.
[141] I Cor. 16.21; Gal. 6.11; Col. 4.18; II Thess. 3.17.

of chapter 16: many insert it at the end of chapter 14 instead: some at the end of chapter 15: others have it twice, once at the end of 14 and again at the end of 16; and yet others omit it altogether.

From all this (and more) it is plain that the Epistle circulated in the early Church, sometimes as a letter addressed to Christians generally, and sometimes without one or both of the last two chapters. But chapters 15 and 16 were unquestionably written by St. Paul. The problem, therefore, is, Did St. Paul write only one version of the Epistle, which he despatched to Rome, and then other people edit it afterwards, or was he himself responsible for more than one edition?

Most prefer the first alternative and suggest reasons why later editors have tampered with the original. Thus, it may have been thought advisable to give so important a doctrinal statement a wider application than it would seem to have if addressed only to a particular church. The heretic Marcion[142] may have detected contradictions between chapter 15 and his own theological theories and have excised chapters 14 and 16 accordingly. Or the long list of salutations in chapter 16 may have been found unsuitable for reading in church and have been omitted in copies designed for liturgical use.

If we prefer the second alternative we may suppose either that St. Paul wrote first a general treatise on the relations between Jews and Gentiles in their new-found faith in Christ, and then later, because he thought it was suitable, sent a special edition of it as a letter to Rome; or that he first wrote the Epistle as we know it, and then later took out the particular references in order to make it applicable to Christians everywhere.

If, in addition, we are convinced by those who maintain that chapter 16 does not belong to Romans at all, but was originally an independent note (though probably written at the same time) commending Phoebe to the church at Ephesus,[143] the number of possibilities is increased still further, since this suggestion may be com-

---

[142] On Marcion and his activities as an editor of the New Testament, see below, pp. 145-7, 150.

[143] The main reasons for this view are: (1) there are more personal greetings in Rom. 16 than in any other of St. Paul's epistles, and it is odd that he should have known so many members of a church he had never visited; (2) Epaenetus is referred to as 'the first-fruits of Asia', in which province Ephesus was the scene of the first Christian mission; and (3) greetings are sent to Prisca and Aquila, who seem to have settled permanently at Ephesus after St. Paul left them there on his second journey (cp. Acts 18.19-21; I Cor. 16.19; II Tim. 4.19).

bined in a variety of different ways with either of the above alternatives. Yet whatever may be the true solution, there can be no doubt whatever that St. Paul, while on his last visit to Corinth, did in fact address a letter to Rome, which is in all essentials the Epistle as it stands in our Bibles to-day.

At the conclusion of his three months' stay in Corinth St. Paul departed on his final journey to Jerusalem by way of Macedonia[144] and the sea route along the coast of Asia Minor and Syria, landing eventually at Caesarea.[145] In Jerusalem he was well received by ' the brethren ', and not only reported on the progress of the Gentile Mission,[146] but also presented the offerings of his converts as a token of their good will towards their mother-church.[147] But he soon got into trouble with the Jerusalem Jews. Raising a cry that he had ' brought Gentiles into the temple ' and ' defiled this holy place ' they gathered a hostile mob against him, from which he was only rescued with difficulty by the timely intervention of the Roman tribune.[148] So began the lengthy period of captivity.

An examination the next day before the Jerusalem ' council ' resulted in another tumult, and St. Paul was withdrawn for safety ' into the castle '.[149] The discovery of a cunningly laid plot against his life induced the tribune to send him under escort to the pro-curator at Caesarea.[150] There he remained for three years, still a prisoner, until in desperation he ' appealed unto Caesar '.[151] This involved a journey by sea to Rome. On the journey his ship was wrecked and he was all but drowned.[152] But at last he set foot in the Imperial City, and was ' suffered to abide by himself with the soldier that guarded him '.[153] The opportunity thus afforded he eagerly seized for preaching. To his lodging he summoned the leaders of the Roman Jews,[154] some of whom he converted.[155] Doubtless Gentiles came as well.[156] And, of course, a continual stream of Christians.[157]

It is at this point that the narrative in Acts stops short. Tradition affirms that St. Paul was martyred in the persecution which broke out under the Emperor Nero in 64. Some writers hold the view that the martyrdom did not follow immediately on the cap-

[144] Acts 20.3.
[145] Acts 21.8.
[146] Acts 21.19.
[147] Acts 24.17.
[148] Acts 21.27-22.29.
[149] Acts 22.30-23.10.
[150] Acts 23.12-35.
[151] Acts 24.1-26.32.
[152] Acts 27.1-44.
[153] Acts 28.16.
[154] Acts 28.17ff.
[155] Acts 28.24.
[156] Acts 28.28.
[157] Acts 28.30.

tivity recorded in Acts. At the end of two years (his ' first Roman captivity '), they say, St. Paul was tried, acquitted, and released : he then embarked on fresh missionary activities; and then, later, was re-arrested, brought back to Rome (his ' second Roman captivity '), condemned, and executed. Whether this was so or not we shall never know.[158] It is best, therefore, to refuse to speculate and take leave of St. Paul, the prisoner in Rome, in the closing words of Acts :

' And he abode two whole years in his own hired dwelling, and received all that went in unto him, preaching the kingdom of God, and teaching the things concerning the Lord Jesus Christ with all boldness, none forbidding him.'

[158] For a brief discussion of this possibility, see below, pp. 74-6.

Chapter Three

ST. PAUL AND HIS
EPISTLES (II)

IN THE PREVIOUS chapter we sketched the main events of St. Paul's life as a Christian and set four of his epistles in what is generally agreed to be their proper contexts. In this chapter we shall be concerned with the remaining ten 'Pauline' epistles.

These ten have been reserved for separate treatment because each in its own way presents a special problem. Sometimes it is the claim of a particular epistle to be a genuine letter written by St. Paul himself that is in dispute: sometimes it is the setting of an epistle which is undoubtedly genuine in its proper context. And since the problems involved are so diverse we shall, for the most part, adopt the expedient of taking each epistle separately. First, the special problem which each presents will be fairly stated: next, the more convincing of the solutions that have been proposed will be briefly passed in review; and finally, wherever possible, an attempt will be made to indicate which of the solutions proposed is the most probable.

II Thessalonians

This epistle is strikingly similar to I Thessalonians. According to the opening salutation it is sent by 'Paul and Silvanus and Timothy',[1] as is I Thessalonians;[2] and these are the only two instances of the name of Silvanus (= Silas) being coupled with that of St. Paul in any of the Pauline salutations. Moreover, in both epistles the situations presumed and the subjects treated are almost identical. Just as in the First Epistle St. Paul opens with a reference to the persecution at Thessalonica and the 'afflictions' that his converts were called upon to endure, so also in the Second; and again

[1] II Thess. 1.1.   [2] I Thess. 1.1.

he commends them for standing firm.[3]   Just as in the First Epistle
he feels compelled in view of current misconceptions to give more
precise instruction on the fundamental hope of the primitive Gospel
(i.e. the coming of the Day), so also in the Second he explains in
greater detail ' the coming of our Lord Jesus Christ and our gathering
together unto him'.[4]   There are the same strictures, too, in both
epistles on those at Thessalonica who were using the hope as an
excuse for idleness; and there are the same positive commands to
the church as a whole to see that every member does his share of
daily toil, as St. Paul himself when among them had taught them
both by precept and example.[5]   And very much the same words
and phrases are used in each case.

If the Second Epistle is genuine there can be no doubt that it was
written at approximately the same time as the First Epistle—that
is, during St. Paul's stay of eighteen months at Corinth on his
second journey.   And since there are two references in it to an
' epistle', apparently emanating from St. Paul, by which the
Thessalonians either had been, or might be, influenced,[6] it must
presumably be dated after, though not very long after, the First
Epistle.

But the Epistle's genuineness has been questioned.   Details apart,
it is alleged that the teaching about the End in the two epistles is
so radically different that it is impossible to suppose that they could
have been written by the same man within a comparatively short
space of time.   In the First Epistle, it is said, St. Paul looks forward
to the coming of the Day as imminent: in the Second it is more
distant—in fact the writer goes out of his way to make it plain that
a great deal has to happen first.   ' Now we beseech you, brethren
. . .', he writes, ' that ye be not quickly shaken from your mind,
nor yet be troubled, either by spirit, or by word, or by epistle as
from us, as though the day of the Lord is just at hand.'[7]   Such a
contrast, it is maintained, is only explicable if we suppose that the
two epistles are by different authors.   The suggestion is, therefore,
that sometime after St. Paul's death, one of his disciples, realizing
that the account of the End given in the First Epistle (notably St.
Paul's expectation that he himself would be alive when the End
came)[8] had been falsified by events, and, jealous of his master's
honour, deliberately wrote the Second Epistle in St. Paul's name,

[3] II Thess. 1.3-6.   [4] II Thess. 2.1-12.   [5] II Thess. 3.6-15.
[6] II Thess. 2.2,15.   [7] II Thess. 2.1,2.   [8] I Thess. 4.15.

his object being, by following closely the outline and even the phraseology of the genuine First Epistle, yet by substituting a more up-to-date and satisfactory exposition of the teaching about the End such as would appear to be St. Paul's own 'second thoughts' on this crucial issue, to save him from discredit in the eyes of a later age. And the suggestion is supported further, partly by interpreting the warning to the Thessalonians not to be 'quickly shaken' or 'troubled' by what they found in any 'epistle as from us'[7] as a thinly veiled attack on the teaching of the First Epistle, and partly by taking II Thess. 3.17 ('The salutation of me Paul with mine own hand, which is the token in every epistle') as the writer's concluding attempt to give an air of verisimilitude to what he knew very well was not a genuine letter signed with St. Paul's own hand.[9]

Such arguments are weighty. And if it be assumed that St. Paul's ideas were static, and that he set down precisely everything that was in his mind on any matter each time he had occasion to write about it, they would seem to be decisive. But St. Paul's ideas were not static: nor did he (any more than anyone else) say everything he might have said whenever he wrote a letter. St. Paul wrote his letters with particular readers in view in particular situations. There is in consequence nothing improbable in supposing that in this instance, after the despatch of I Thessalonians, he heard that its effects were insufficient: that he was told that there were still many at Thessalonica who ignored his warnings against idleness, and that they were encouraged, rather than the reverse, by what he had written about the End. So he writes again to warn them with greater sternness, making it plain at the same time that the End, though shortly to come to pass, is not immediate. They must wait for it in patience, and, meanwhile, 'work and eat their bread' in 'quietness' as he had told them when he was with them.[10]

Viewed from this angle the arguments against the genuineness of the Epistle lose most of their force. That the Epistle presents difficulties no one will deny. But the difficulties are not insurmountable if we remember, first that St. Paul was human and that the Thessalonians were human too, and secondly that while fully occupied with his work in Corinth he had to deal by letter only with a very troublesome situation at Thessalonica which developed from day to day.

[9] On St. Paul's practice in this respect, see above, p. 51.
[10] II Thess. 3.12,10.

Galatians

About the genuineness of Galatians there is no dispute. The problems here are destination and date. As a preliminary, however, it will be as well to note that the Epistle differs from all the other Pauline Epistles addressed to churches in that it is addressed, not to any one church, but to a group of churches—'the churches of Galatia'.[11]

When St. Paul first preached in this area he had been well received.[12]   But after his departure others had followed in his footsteps and had preached 'a different gospel', impugning both his authority and his message, and 'bewitching' his converts by the 'correctness' of their teaching.[13]   These people were clearly circumcisionists.[14]   And St. Paul deals with the situation (it seems as soon as he heard about it) in a letter, which, more than any other, shows the impulsiveness of his nature.

His authority, he declares, is not from men but from God.[15] His Gospel is not the product of his own imagination: it is the Gospel that he was divinely commissioned to preach when he was converted.[16]   And if it be suggested that the acknowledged leaders of the Church do not approve of his activities, then their attitude towards him when visiting Jerusalem should be sufficient to silence such a suggestion: indeed, when on his last visit he had brought up this very question in case they might not approve, he had received from St. James, St. Peter, and St. John, the reputed 'pillars' of the Church, not only complete approval of his Gospel, but also 'the right hand of fellowship' for his work among the Gentiles.[17]

Then, after describing how the question was further thrashed out with St. Peter at Antioch,[18] St. Paul launches[19] into the main argument of the Epistle, that 'a man is not justified by the works of the law but through faith in Jesus Christ' and that 'with freedom did Christ set us free' from the 'yoke of bondage' of Judaism[20] —the same argument that we have already followed in a more systematic form in Romans. Next come some general exhorta-

---

[11] Gal. 1.2.
[14] Gal. 4.21; 5.2; 6.12.
[17] Gal. 1.18-2.10.
[12] Gal. 4.12-15.
[15] Gal. 1.1.
[18] Gal. 2.11-15.
[13] Gal. 1.6-10; 3.1.
[16] Gal. 1.11-17.
[19] The transition is a good illustration of St. Paul's impulsiveness. There is no break at all between what he says he said to St. Peter at Antioch and what he is now saying to the Galatians. Strictly interpreted, the whole of the rest of the Epistle is a record of what he said to St. Peter!   [20] Gal. 2.16-5.12.

tions.[21]   And then St. Paul adds a few final words with his own hand,[22] reverting again to the circumcision question, and concluding with the plea, 'From henceforth let no man trouble me: for I bear branded on my body the marks of Jesus.'

Who were these Galatians?

There are two possibilities.   Either they were the descendants of the Celtic warriors, who at the beginning of the third century B.C. had settled in northern Asia Minor, in the neighbourhood of the modern Ankara, and in St. Paul's day still remained very much a separate people; or they were the inhabitants of the Roman province of Galatia, which, established in 25 B.C., embraced not only the district inhabited by the Galatians proper, but also a considerable tract of territory situated to the south, including among other towns, Pisidian Antioch, Iconium, Lystra, and Derbe.   The choice, then, is between insisting on the narrower ethnographic interpretation of 'Galatians' and being prepared to give it a wider political connotation.

Unfortunately Acts gives very little direct assistance.   Nowhere in Acts is there any record of St. Paul's having preached to 'Galatians', although on two occasions there are casual references to 'Galatia'.   On the first occasion St. Paul is said to have 'gone through the region of Phrygia and Galatia' on his way through Asia Minor at the beginning of his second journey;[23] and again, he 'went through the region of Galatia and Phrygia' when he started on his third.[24]   Both passages, when read in their contexts, imply the revisiting of churches already founded.   It is most natural, therefore, to take 'Galatia' in both passages in the political sense (i.e. as referring to the Roman province), and to suppose that St. Paul was going over again the ground he had covered on his first journey.   In this case 'the churches of Galatia' in the Epistle will be the churches of South Galatia, with which we are familiar from Acts—Antioch, Iconium, Lystra, and Derbe.   If, on the other hand, we press the strictly ethnographical interpretation of 'Galatians' and maintain that St. Paul was writing to certain Celtic churches in North Galatia, then we shall have to acknowledge that, apart from two bare notices in Acts of St. Paul's having visited them in passing on his second and third journeys, and from what may be inferred from the Epistle, we know nothing whatever about either their foundation or their history.

[21] Gal. 5.13-6.10.   [22] Gal. 6.11-18.   [23] Acts 16.6.   [24] Acts 18.23.

Those who prefer the North Galatian destination usually suppose that the churches were founded on the second journey. They suggest that after visiting the churches of South Galatia,[25] St. Paul deserted the main road which continued into the province of Asia, and turned northwards to undertake evangelistic work in what nowadays would be called the 'backwoods' of the Galatian uplands;[26] and they explain the glossing over in Acts of St. Paul's pioneer work there as due either to the author's ignorance of what had really happened, or to his thinking that the foundation of such out-of-the-way churches was unworthy of record. On this view the date of the Epistle must at the earliest be later than the first few months of the second journey. In the Epistle itself, however, St. Paul speaks of his cordial reception when he 'preached the gospel' among the Galatians 'the first [R.V. margin "former"] time'.[27] At the time of writing, therefore, St. Paul must have paid the Galatians at least two visits; and the second is to be identified with the visit mentioned in Acts at the beginning of the third journey. Hence, it is argued, the Epistle must have been written after this. Most incline to a date somewhere towards the end of the third journey, either in the latter part of the two years' stay at Ephesus, or during the tour of Macedonia and Greece before the final visit to Jerusalem.

If we prefer the South Galatian destination this late date is equally possible. But there is one major difficulty in the way of a late date. Acts 15 gives a full account of a council of 'apostles and elders' at Jerusalem held soon after St. Paul's return from his first journey, and summoned to discuss the very point with which St. Paul is concerned in the Epistle—namely, to what extent, if at all, Gentile converts were bound by the specifically Jewish practices of primitive Palestinian Christianity. The result was a decision, as we have seen,[28] substantially in St. Paul's favour. The decision was embodied in a decree; and the decree was not only accepted with acclamation at Antioch where the problem had first become acute,[29] but also 'delivered . . . for to keep' by St. Paul himself to the churches of South Galatia when he started on his second journey.[30] If, then, the Epistle was written after the promulgation of the decree, it is extraordinary (to say the least) that St. Paul, when called upon to defend both his Gospel and his authority

[25] Acts 16.1-5.   [26] Acts 16.6.   [27] Gal. 4.13.
[28] See above, p. 25.   [29] Acts 15.30.   [30] Acts 16.4.

against the attacks of circumcisionists, should not mention it to the very people to whom he is said to have delivered it. To take his stand on the decree would have been, of course, the most complete answer he could have given.

It seems, therefore, that there are good grounds for dating the Epistle before the Jerusalem Council. While St. Paul was at Antioch at the conclusion of his first journey 'certain men came down from Judaea and taught the brethren, saying, Except ye be circumcised after the custom of Moses, ye cannot be saved'.[31] We shall infer that they had also penetrated as far as the newly founded churches in South Galatia, where they were creating a serious disturbance. St. Paul immediately takes counter-measures. Amid the 'no small dissension and questioning' at Antioch[32] he writes to the Galatians 'a piece of his mind'; and soon afterwards departs with St. Barnabas and the others to argue his case at Jerusalem. The contents of the Epistle fit this situation admirably. If it be objected that St. Paul, when he wrote, had visited the Galatians twice, we may reply that this idea depends on a mistranslation—the Greek word translated 'the first time' at Gal. 4.13 means as often as not 'at one time' or 'originally',[33] and no second visit is implied. Thus interpreted the Epistle is St. Paul's first literary missile in a long and bitter controversy; it is also the earliest of his surviving letters.

THE CAPTIVITY EPISTLES

The term 'captivity epistles' is by common consent applied to the four epistles in which St. Paul seems to write from prison —Ephesians, Philippians, Colossians, and Philemon; and since the 'captivity' references[34] inevitably mark these four off from the other Pauline letters it is convenient to treat them as a group.

But we must be careful that our approach to them as a group, merely because they share 'captivity' references in common, does not lead us to assume without further investigation that they share anything else in common. We must not assume, for example, that they are one and all either genuine or not genuine: nor, again, that if genuine, they are all to be assigned to the same date, place,

---

[31] Acts 15.1.   [32] Acts 15.2.
[33] Cp. e.g. I Tim. 1.13: 'though I was *before* a blasphemer and a persecutor'.
[34] Eph. 3.1; 4.1; 6.20; Phil. 1.7,13,14,17; Col. 4.3,10,18; Philem. 1,9,10,13.

or set of circumstances.   St. Paul himself reminds the Corinthians that he had been in prison more than once.[35]   He was very possibly arrested and imprisoned (perhaps for quite a time) at Ephesus.[36] And Acts makes it certain that he was a prisoner for no less than three years at Caesarea,[37] and later for at least two years in Rome.[38] There are, therefore, several possible contexts in which a 'captivity epistle' may be set.

Colossians and Philemon

Colossians and Philemon unquestionably belong together.   In both St. Timothy's name is coupled with St. Paul's in the opening address.[39]   In both Aristarchus, Mark, Epaphras, Luke and Demas, all appear in the concluding salutations as St. Paul's 'fellow-workers', who together with him send their greetings.[40]   In both Archippus is mentioned (the only two times he is mentioned): in Colossians he is to be given a message;[41] in Philemon he is named alongside Philemon and Apphia in the opening address.[42]   Onesi-mus, too, whose return to his master forms the main topic of Philemon,[43] is only referred to elsewhere at Col. 4.9, where he is said to be 'one of' the Colossians and consequently able to tell them by word of mouth anything about St. Paul that had not found a place in the letter.   Both epistles, therefore, were written, and presumably despatched, at the same time, the one being addressed to the Colossian church as a whole, the other being an accompanying private note to an individual member.

Colossae was situated in the valley of the River Lycus in the Roman province of Asia, about eighty miles east of Ephesus.   St. Paul had never been there.[44]   The Colossians had heard the Gospel from Epaphras, who had also worked in the neighbouring towns of Hierapolis and Laodicea.[45]   The date of these churches' foundation cannot with certainty be determined; but we may very plausibly fix it during St. Paul's two-year stay at Ephesus on his third journey, when 'all they which dwelt in Asia heard the word of the Lord, both Jews and Greeks'.[46]   Consequently, even though St. Paul had not founded the churches himself, they were the result

[35] II Cor. 11.23.
[36] The enigmatic reference in I Cor. 15.32 is frequently so interpreted.
[37] Acts 23.23-26.32.   [38] Acts 28.30.   [39] Col. 1.1; Philem. 1.
[40] Col. 4.10-14; Philem. 23,24.   [41] Col. 4.17.   [42] Philem. 2.
[43] Philem. 1off.   [44] Col. 2.1.   [45] Col. 1.5-7; 4.12,13.
[46] Acts 19.10.

of his activity in the provincial capital, and he could justifiably regard them as his own.

At the time of writing Epaphras was with St. Paul,[47] and he had reported on the Colossians' progress.[48]   On the whole the report was encouraging;[49] but there was evidently not a little trouble occasioned by false teachers.[50]   So St. Paul writes a message of reassurance, urging his readers to remain steadfast in the faith they had been taught.[51]   The Gospel, he reminds them, is centred in Christ.[52]   They must take care, therefore, that no one ' delude ' them by ' persuasiveness of speech ': neither extreme ascetic practices nor excessive devotion to angels are part of the true Gospel: such things belong to ' the rudiments of the world ' and are ' precepts and doctrines of men ', which should be powerless to ensnare the believer who is ' risen with Christ '.[53]   By contrast, the Risen Life in Christ has a quality all its own; and St. Paul expands this point in a final section consisting of specific practical exhortations.[54]

The Epistle was sent off by Tychicus, who, together with Onesimus, was charged with ' making known ' to the Colossians, not only St. Paul's personal affairs, but also everything else that was going on in his place of captivity.[55]   Besides this we need only note a verse very near the end—' And when this epistle hath been read among you, cause that it be read also in the church of the Laodiceans; and that ye also read the epistle from Laodicea.'[56]

What was this ' epistle from Laodicea ' with which St. Paul recommends the Colossians to exchange their own epistle?

Some identify it with a letter headed ' The Epistle to the Laodiceans ', which is found in not a few Latin manuscripts of the Pauline epistles, though not in any Greek manuscript, and not, of course, in our English Bibles.   Others identify it with Ephesians. Yet others suppose the reference to be to an epistle actually written to the Laodiceans at the same time as Colossians and Philemon, but not now extant.   Whatever may be the truth of the matter, of one thing we may be sure—that ' The Epistle to the Laodiceans ' of the Latin manuscripts is a forgery, produced in order to provide an easy answer to our question.   The effective choice is thus between the second and third alternatives.   The case for the identification

[47] Col. 4.12.　　　　　[48] Col. 1.8.　　　　　[49] Col. 1.4.
[50] Col. 2.8ff.　　　　　[51] Col. 2.5-7.　　　　　[52] Col. 1.15-2.3.
[53] Col. 2.4-3.4.　　　　[54] Col. 3.5-4.6.　　　　[55] Col. 4.7-9.
[56] Col. 4.16.

with Ephesians is best left until later.[57] Meanwhile, we may reflect that there is no reason whatever for supposing that all St. Paul's letters have been preserved (on the contrary, there is every reason against doing so), and it is therefore highly probable that the original Laodiceans is one of those that have been lost.

The note to Philemon concerns Onesimus. Onesimus was a slave of Philemon's[58] who had run away and had been converted to Christianity by St. Paul in prison.[59] St. Paul now sends him back to his master[60] and asks that he may be kindly received, both because he is now a ' brother ' Christian, and also because he himself has a high regard for him.[61] St. Paul adds that he is ready to reimburse Philemon out of his own pocket for any theft Onesimus may have committed or any debt that he may owe.[62] And he further asks Philemon to ' prepare a lodging ' against his own release, when he has the fullest intention of coming to Colossae himself.[63]

It is improbable that these epistles were written from Caesarea. A runaway slave from Asia is hardly likely to have fled to Palestine; while St. Paul, throughout his captivity at Caesarea, seems to have kept his eyes so firmly fixed on Rome and the West[64] that he can scarcely have hoped to visit Colossae for a very long time to come —in which case his request to Philemon to ' prepare a lodging ' for him takes on an air of unreality. On the other hand, Rome, the populous and cosmopolitan capital of the Empire, was exactly the sort of place to which the fugitive Onesimus would be attracted: at Rome he might very easily be drawn into the circle that ' went in ' to St. Paul ' in his own hired dwelling ' and be converted; while St. Paul, for his part, might very well hope towards the end of ' two whole years ' there shortly to be set at liberty and so in a position to follow Onesimus to Colossae. We must, of course, reckon with the possibility that the epistles were written from Ephesus : that it was to Ephesus, to the provincial capital, that Onesimus fled; and that it was from Ephesus that St. Paul hoped soon to be able to visit one of the outlying churches of the province. Attractive, however, as this possibility is, it can never be more than a possibility, since there is no direct evidence that St. Paul was ever in prison at Ephesus. If we desire the safest solution in the light of what we know for certain, that solution must be Rome.

[57] See below, p. 70.   [58] Philem. 16.   [59] Philem. 10.   [60] Philem. 12.
[61] Philem. 16,17.   [62] Philem. 18,19.   [63] Philem. 22.
[64] Acts 19.21; Rom. 1.15; 15.22-29; Acts 23.11; 25.11,12.

Philippians

Philippi was the capital of the province of Macedonia, and the church there was founded by St. Paul on his second journey. The details are described at length in Acts 16.12-40. It further appears from Acts that St. Paul revisited Philippi twice on the third journey;[65] and the Epistle makes it clear that he had kept in touch in the interim. More than once the Philippians had sent him gifts of money. 'Ye yourselves know,' he writes, 'that in the beginning of the gospel, when I departed from Macedonia, no church had fellowship with me in the matter of giving and receiving but ye only; for even in Thessalonica ye sent once and again unto my need.'[66] But the Philippians' generosity was not confined to 'the beginning of the gospel'. When he wrote the Epistle St. Paul had only recently received yet another proof of their interest in his welfare; and his primary purpose in writing was to thank them for this latest contribution, sent by their 'messenger' Epaphroditus.[67]

'I thank my God upon all my remembrance of you,' St. Paul begins, 'always in every supplication of mine on behalf of you all making my supplication with joy, for your fellowship in furtherance of the gospel from the first day until now.'[68] And this note of thankfulness and joy is sustained throughout the Epistle.[69] There was much in the writer's outward circumstances that might have induced a mood of depression. He was himself a prisoner[70] in 'affliction',[71] not knowing what might be in store for him[72]— very probably the issue might be death.[73] Epaphroditus had been taken ill soon after his arrival and had nearly died.[74] The Philippians, too, from all reports, seemed to be in danger of yielding to the attacks of the circumcisionists from without,[75] while as individuals they were often far removed from that 'lowliness of mind' and consideration for one another which were the hall-marks of the true Christian.[76]

But St. Paul does not despair. The Philippians' danger and failings are the subject of exhortations to which he knows they will give heed.[77] Epaphroditus has through God's mercy at last been restored to health and is returning to Philippi—presumably with the Epistle.[78] And even St. Paul's own imprisonment has turned

[65] Acts 20.2,6.
[66] Phil. 4.15,16.
[67] Phil. 2.25; 4.18.
[68] Phil. 1.3-5.
[69] e.g. Phil. 1.18; 2.2; 3.3; 4.4.
[70] Phil. 1.7,13,14,17.
[71] Phil. 4.14.
[72] Phil. 2.23.
[73] Phil. 1.20; 2.17.
[74] Phil. 2.26,27,30.
[75] Phil. 3.2ff.
[76] Phil. 2.2ff.
[77] Phil. 3.2-4.1; 2.1-18.
[78] Phil. 2.25,28.

E

out 'rather unto the progress of the gospel', in as much as many new converts have been made as a result of his 'bonds'.[79] In all ways, therefore, he rejoices. His readers' latest gift has filled his heart full to overflowing.[80] The issue of life and death seems somehow strangely impersonal.[81] As soon as there is something definite to report he will send St. Timothy after Epaphroditus to Philippi with the news.[82] And if he is spared he hopes also to come himself.[83]

This last hope of St. Paul's, that soon he may be released and able to visit Philippi, recalls the similar hope of a not too far distant visit to Colossae expressed at the end of Philemon.[84] Consequently, one of the objections previously noted to Caesarea as the place of origin of Colossians and Philemon is equally valid for Philippians —namely, that at Caesarea St. Paul looked forward so anxiously to 'seeing' Rome and the West that he is unlikely to have contemplated an excursion elsewhere first. For excursion it must have become, and not just a flying visit to a single local church. A visit to Philippi must inevitably have entailed visits to other churches in the area as well. And, if we maintain in addition that Colossians, Philemon, and Philippians, were all written from Caesarea, the difficulty is proportionately increased. We have, in short, to grant that St. Paul so completely altered his original programme as to substitute an extended tour, not only of Macedonia (and perhaps Achaea too), but also of Asia Minor, for his declared intention to go to Rome—a tour, which, if carried out, must have been so extended as to have been known to posterity as his 'Fourth Missionary Journey'! It seems, then, that we must choose between Ephesus and Rome.

For Ephesus a fair case can be made out. We know from Acts that while at Ephesus on his third journey St. Paul projected a visit to Macedonia, and that he subsequently carried his project into effect.[85] We know also from both Acts and I Corinthians that St. Timothy was with him at the time, and that he was used as a messenger between St. Paul and his churches.[86] It is against this background, accordingly, that many would set St. Paul's half-promise to the Philippians to send Timothy to them, and his hope of being soon able to come himself. The trouble is, of course, that

[79] Phil. 1.12-18.   [80] Phil. 4.18.   [81] Phil. 1.21-23.
[82] Phil. 2.19-23.   [83] Phil. 1.26; 2.24.   [84] Philem. 22.
[85] Acts 19.21,22; 20.1,2. [86] Acts 19.22; I Cor. 4.17; 16.10.

while Philippians was certainly written from prison, we cannot be sure that St. Paul ever was imprisoned at Ephesus. An Ephesian origin for the Epistle can therefore never be more than a distinct possibility.

For Rome the case is much stronger. Although St. Paul writes as a prisoner, he is a prisoner who is allowed considerable freedom: he can receive those who wish to see him : he can carry on correspondence unhindered : he can send out what emissaries he will; and he finds that his apparently unfortunate predicament has ' fallen out rather unto the progress of the gospel '—surely a reflection of the situation described in Acts 28.30,31. There are, furthermore, two definite references which point to Rome rather than anywhere else. When informing the Philippians of his condition, St. Paul remarks that his ' bonds ' have become ' manifest in Christ throughout the whole praetorian guard ';[87] and in the final salutations he includes a special greeting from ' them that are of Caesar's household '.[88] We cannot deny that a detachment of the Imperial bodyguard may have been quartered at Ephesus (or for that matter at Caesarea) at the time; nor can we deny that some members of the Emperor's household may have followed in their wake. But both references read more naturally if we suppose that St. Paul was writing from Rome, and that the Gospel was beginning, even then, to gain adherents among the court. We must allow some time, both for the development of St. Paul's missionary activities after his arrival in Rome, and also for the commissioning of Epaphroditus, his journey, his illness, and his recovery, as well as for the fact that St. Paul had heard that the news of his illness had reached Philippi.[89] Moreover, St. Paul's words about his own ultimate fate breathe an air, as it were, of finality.[90] Thus, the Epistle is best dated in the second year of the Roman captivity—most probably towards the end.

Ephesians

This Epistle raises more, and more awkward, problems than any other epistle so far considered.

After the opening salutation there follows a benediction, which leads immediately into a long and closely knit doctrinal exposition of the divine plan for the redemption of mankind through Christ.[91]

[87] Phil. 1.13.
[90] Phil. 1.21-23.
[88] Phil. 4.22.
[91] Eph. 1.3-3.19.
[89] Phil. 2.26.

That plan, pre-determined before Creation[92] and kept secret through the ages,[93] has now at last been revealed.[94]   Through God's free gift of grace[95] both writer and readers have been enlightened : [96] they have been raised with Christ from the deadness of their former lives of sin and ' made to sit with him in the heavenly places '.[97] But the special point of this new revelation is the unity of Jew and Gentile which has been accomplished in the Church.   Christ, by His death, has broken down ' the middle wall of partition ' between the two, and ' made both one '.[98]   Gentiles are therefore no longer ' strangers and sojourners ' in ' the household of God ',[99] but ' fellow-heirs ' with Jews and ' fellow members of the body '.[100]   This is the Gospel which St. Paul has been commissioned to preach, particularly among the Gentiles; [101] and the exposition concludes with a prayer that God may grant the readers an ever-deepening apprehension of the mystery and an ever-fuller understanding of the real meaning of Christian love.[102]

Two verses of doxology intervene.[103]   And then St. Paul passes to exhortation.[104]   The Ephesians are to ' walk worthily ' of their Christian calling.[105]   They are to exhibit meekness and forbearance to one another : [106] they are to keep the unity of the Church unsullied, remembering always that each member has his appointed place and function in the body as a whole;[107] and as, when they were converted, they turned their backs once for all on ' the unfruitful works of darkness ' they must be perpetually on their guard against any temptation to relapse.[108]   The various family and household relationships are treated one by one.[109]   Next comes another injunction to stand fast in the truth as it has been received.[110]   St. Paul asks his readers to pray for him, that he, a prisoner, may be given ' boldness ' to preach the Gospel.[111]   He sends Tychicus ' the beloved brother and faithful minister in the Lord ' to tell them whatever they may want to know about himself and his condition.[112]   And then he commends them finally to the grace of God.[113]

From the fact that St. Paul was in captivity when writing,[114]

[92] Eph. 1.4.
[93] Eph. 3.5,9.
[94] Eph. 1.9; 3.3,5,10.
[95] Eph. 2.8,9.
[96] Eph. 1.18; 3.3.
[97] Eph. 2.1-6.
[98] Eph. 2.14.
[99] Eph. 2.19.
[100] Eph. 3.6.
[101] Eph. 3.9.
[102] Eph. 3.14-19.
[103] Eph. 3.20,21.
[104] Eph. 4.1-6.20.
[105] Eph. 4.1.
[106] Eph. 4.2.
[107] Eph. 4.3-16.
[108] Eph. 4.17-5.21.
[109] Eph. 5.22-6.9.
[110] Eph. 6.10-18.
[111] Eph. 6.19,20.
[112] Eph. 6. 21,22.
[113] Eph. 6.23,24.
[114] Eph. 3.1; 4.1; 6.20.

and from the fact that the reference to Tychicus and his mission is almost verbally identical with Col. 4.7,8, we shall naturally assume that the Epistle was written at the same time as Colossians and Philemon, and taken together with them by Tychicus and Onesimus, who would doubtless pass through Ephesus on their journey to Colossae.

It is at this point, however, that our first problem presents itself. Apart from St. Paul's mention of his captivity and the reference to Tychicus, there are no personal details whatever. There are none of the customary greetings. Nor does the Epistle appear to have been called forth by any particular event or series of events—indeed it reads much more like a treatise than a letter. There is no reason, of course, why St. Paul should not have written such a treatise. We have already seen that he wrote something very like a treatise to Rome. But the odd thing is that he should have written one to Ephesus. Rome was a special case. St. Paul had never been to Rome: he had not founded the church there: he expressly disclaimed any intention of 'building on another man's foundation';[115] and he obviously thought a general statement of his theological position most suitable in the circumstances. Yet even these considerations did not restrain him from including in Romans not a little personal detail,[116] and (if Rom. 16 really belongs to Romans)[117] the best part of a chapter of individual greetings. At Ephesus, however, the situation was different. St. Paul was the founder of the Ephesian church:[118] he had stayed there for between two and three years on his third journey and been the leader of an extremely successful mission;[119] and on his last pilgrimage to Jerusalem he had sent for the Ephesian elders to Miletus and admonished them to keep their trust.[120] His circle of acquaintance in Ephesus must therefore have been immense, and his ties of friendship with many very close. In consequence, the calm and detached tone of the Epistle, combined with the almost complete absence of personal detail, is nothing short of astounding.

To some extent our second problem may provide an answer to the first. As the Revised Version notes in the margin at Eph. 1.1, 'some very ancient authorities' omit the words 'at Ephesus'. Furthermore, the second-century heretic Marcion[121] referred to

[115] Rom. 15.20.   [116] Rom. 15.14-29.   [117] See above, p. 52.
[118] Acts 18.19.   [119] Acts 19.1-20.1.   [120] Acts 20.17-38.
[121] On the importance of Marcion, see below, pp. 145-7, 150.

Ephesians habitually as Laodiceans. Thus, there was obviously some doubt in the early Church about the Epistle's destination. But the question that concerns us is, For whom did St. Paul originally intend it, and what did he himself write in the opening verse?

Four solutions are possible:

(1) That St. Paul intended the Epistle for Ephesus and addressed it to Ephesus, but someone else later cut out the original address (and perhaps also some personal detail) in order to give it a more general application for use in the Church at large—in this case Marcion's ascription of it to Laodicea is presumably an astute guess that the edited 'general' epistle, clearly very closely associated with Colossians, is to be identified with the enigmatic 'epistle from Laodicea' mentioned at Col. 4.16.

(2) That, as before, St. Paul addressed the Epistle to Ephesus, but Marcion deliberately substituted Laodicea because he had quarrelled with the church authorities at Ephesus and thought that Laodicea, a church with an admittedly bad reputation,[122] was in the circumstances a most effective substitute—in this case the 'general' version may either have been derived from the original independently in the manner suggested above, or else be the result of anti-Marcionite expurgation.

(3) That Ephesians is in fact 'the epistle from Laodicea' and that St. Paul addressed it there himself, but either because a more general address was later thought necessary, or because of the bad odour into which the church of Laodicea had fallen, the original address was removed, some copies being left without any address at all, and Ephesus being substituted in others—in this case Marcion will have preserved the correct address.

(4) That at the same time as he wrote Colossians and Philemon, St. Paul wrote also a circular letter to all the churches of Asia Minor, leaving a blank in the address to be filled in appropriately: that it was to go first to Laodicea (hence 'the epistle *from* Laodicea' at Col. 4.16) and finish up at Ephesus—in this case Ephesians as it stands in our Bibles to-day will have followed a tradition derived from the copy preserved in the church at Ephesus, the 'very ancient authorities' of the Revised Version margin a tradition derived from St. Paul's autograph, and Marcion one derived from the copy preserved at Laodicea.

Most students, when faced with these alternatives, will prefer

[122] Cp. Rev. 3.15,16.

the last, if for no other reason than that it alone provides a satisfactory explanation, both of the Epistle's detached and general tone, and also of the absence of the customary personal details.   But now comes our final problem, Can we be sure that the Epistle is genuine?

An increasing body of opinion nowadays is inclined to answer 'No'.   It is pointed out that a number of words and phrases occur in the Epistle which do not occur in St. Paul's indisputably genuine epistles: the Evil One, for example, is twice referred to as 'the devil',[123] whereas St. Paul elsewhere calls him 'Satan'.[124]   Some of these words and phrases are characteristic of an age later than St. Paul's and reflect a later stage of doctrinal development: thus, whereas, in using the metaphor of the Church as a building, St. Paul states categorically to the Corinthians 'other foundation can no man lay than that which is laid, which is Jesus Christ',[125] in Ephesians the Church is said to be 'built upon the foundation of the apostles and prophets'.[126]   The over-all difference in style, too, is remarkable: elsewhere St. Paul appears consistently as a vigorous writer, he is normally concerned to drive home particular points, and he often displays himself as a most determined controversialist[127]—so much so that the thread of his thought is frequently very difficult to follow; yet in Ephesians, as one modern author aptly remarks, his thoughts 'move forward with the flow of a deep river'.[128]

Even so, there are very many very close parallels with Colossians,[129] and several fairly close with other epistles.[130]   It is manifestly not inconceivable that St. Paul, towards the end of his life, should have addressed to Asia Minor from Rome a general treatise, summing up, and to some extent developing, his message to the Church at large.   And it is more than likely that, if he did so, his tone would be more detached and his style less controversial than usual, and that he would use at least a few words and phrases that he had not used elsewhere.   But to suggest that he actually did so, and that Ephesians is what he wrote, does scant justice to the evidence.

[123] Eph. 4.27; 6.11.
[124] e.g. Rom. 16.20; I Cor. 5.5; II Cor. 2.11; I Thess. 2.18.
[125] I Cor. 3.11.
[126] Eph. 2.20.
[127] Cp. especially the examination and confutation of an imaginary opponent in Rom. 2.1ff.
[128] A. H. McNeile, St. Paul, p. 218.
[129] e.g. Eph. 1.4 and Col. 1.22; Eph. 1.7 and Col. 1.14.
[130] e.g. Eph. 4.25 and Rom. 12.5; Eph. 4.28 and I Thess. 4.11,12.

Consequently, the Epistle is best explained as the work of one of St. Paul's disciples, who, soaked in his master's teaching, and taking Colossians as his model, wrote in St. Paul's name, for the edification of the Church in his own day, a complete and ordered exposition of the Pauline Gospel. Perhaps his aim in the first instance was to provide a suitable introduction to a collection of St. Paul's letters: perhaps that collection was made at Ephesus—hence the popular ascription 'to the Ephesians'. But here we can only guess. At all events, since Colossians served as a model, the unknown author must have written after the year 65; and, since Ephesians is quoted by St. Clement of Rome in the year 95,[131] it must have been published some years previously. A date between 75 and 80 is as near as we are likely to get.

THE PASTORAL EPISTLES
I Timothy, II Timothy, Titus

These three Epistles, like the Captivity Epistles, fall into a well-defined group on their own. They are called 'pastoral' because in them St. Paul appears as a chief pastor giving direction to his subordinates about the spiritual care of the churches entrusted to their oversight. There are marked similarities between all three in style, form, and content. And, apart from Philemon, they are the only surviving letters attributed to St. Paul that are addressed to individuals.

Their contents can be briefly summarized. Active in the churches for which Timothy and Titus are responsible are men who 'teach a different doctrine'[132] from the traditional and beguile the unwary with new-fangled 'questionings'[133], 'fables',[134] 'genealogies',[135] and the like, which they represent as the essential 'knowledge'[136] which every Christian should possess. But for St Paul it is 'knowledge falsely so called',[136] and those who teach it are 'profane babblers'.[137] Timothy and Titus must therefore be on their guard against such teachers, and energetically repudiate both them and their teaching.[138] They must themselves at all times instil 'sound doctrine',[139] and be shining 'ensamples' to all men,

---

[131] I Clem. 36.2; 46.6.   [132] I Tim. 1.3; 6.3.
[133] I Tim. 1.4; 6.4; II Tim. 2.23; Tit. 3.9.
[134] I Tim. 1.4; 4.7: II Tim. 4.4; Tit. 1.14.
[135] I Tim. 1.4; Tit. 3.9.   [136] I Tim. 6.20.
[137] I Tim. 6.20; II Tim. 2.16.   [138] I Tim. 4.7; II Tim. 2.23; Tit. 3.10.
[139] I Tim. 1.10; II Tim. 4.3; Tit. 2.1.

not only in the 'soundness of their doctrine', but also in their 'good works' and 'manner of life':[140] they must see to it that any who are appointed to any office in their churches are of the right type both doctrinally and morally;[141] and they must inculcate the same pattern of belief and behaviour in the rank and file.[142] Here and there a few personal details are interposed (notably in II Timothy);[143] but otherwise the Epistles are concerned entirely with instructions for the ordering of the life of certain local churches in view of the danger which threatens from false teachers.

What situations do the Epistles reflect, and when were they written?

In I Timothy St. Paul writes that when he was 'going into Macedonia' he had 'exhorted' Timothy 'to tarry at Ephesus'[144] and adds afterwards that he hopes to join him 'shortly'.[145] But there is no correspondence here with any of St. Paul's movements or intentions so far as they are known.

At the time of writing II Timothy St. Paul is in prison[146] at Rome,[147] and his death is imminent.[148] The details given, however, are most provokingly at variance with the details given in Colossians, Philemon, and Philippians, which were in all probability written from Rome. In II Timothy, St. Paul asks Timothy to come to him,[149] and in addition to 'bring Mark' with him:[150] yet when Colossians, Philemon, and Philippians were written, Timothy was with St. Paul,[151] while Mark sends greetings in Colossians and Philemon.[152] It would be tempting, of course, to suppose that II Timothy is to be dated before the others, and that Timothy and Mark had arrived in the interval in accordance with St. Paul's instructions. But this is impossible, for, whereas in Colossians and Philemon a number of greetings are sent, and among them greetings from Luke and Demas,[153] in II Timothy St. Paul laments that he has been left almost completely alone, that Demas especially has 'forsaken' him, and that 'only Luke' is with him[154]—which argues, as plainly as anything can, a later date. And a later date is further supported by the remark 'Tychicus I sent to

[140] I Tim. 4.12; Tit. 2.7.
[141] I Tim. 3.1-13; Tit. 1.5-9.
[142] I Tim. 2.1-15: Tit. 2.1-3.8.
[143] I Tim. 1.3; 3.14; 4.13; II Tim. 1.5,8,15-18; 4.6-21; Tit. 1.5; 3.12-15.
[144] I Tim. 1.3.   [145] I Tim. 3.14; 4.13.   [146] II Tim. 1.8.
[147] II Tim. 1.17.   [148] II Tim. 4.6-8.   [149] II Tim. 4.9,21.
[150] II Tim. 4.11.   [151] Col. 1.1; Philem. 1; Phil. 1.1.   [152] Col. 4.10; Philem. 24.
[153] Col. 4.14; Philem. 24.   [154] II Tim. 4.10,11.

Ephesus[155] (presumably an allusion to the mission of Tychicus mentioned at Col. 4.10), as well as by the certainty which seems to dominate St. Paul's mind that he has 'finished his course' and that 'the time of his departure is come',[156] which contrasts forcibly with the obviously earlier hope of a speedy release expressed in Philemon and Philippians.[157]   There is, in short, a baffling combination of agreement and disagreement; and we can only 'square' the two situations by supposing that at first St. Paul was surrounded in Rome by very many of his friends and lieutenants, that after the despatch of Colossians, Philemon, and Philippians, nearly all of them had either been sent off on various missions or else had drifted away of their own accord, and that later still, when he became convinced that the end was near, he was moved to recall Timothy and Mark in what must consequently be regarded as the last of his extant epistles.   This solution, though, fails to explain the contents of the Epistle.   If St. Paul was writing to recall Timothy and Mark so that they might be with him at the end, we should expect no more than a few lines written with a sense of urgency.   But II Timothy as a whole strikes no note of urgency. On the contrary, it consists mainly of further instruction to Timothy on how to discharge his office of overseer;[158] and it seems to envisage some considerable time elapsing, devoted to quiet and patient labour,[159] before at length Timothy heeds St. Paul's summons.

The case of Titus is similar to that of I Timothy.   Here St. Paul says that he left Titus in Crete 'to set in order the things that are wanting, and appoint elders in every city',[160] and that he himself intends to 'winter' at Nicopolis.[161]   Again the situation described does not fit any known situation in St. Paul's life.

To resolve these difficulties it is frequently suggested that all three Pastoral Epistles belong to a period subsequent to the end of Acts.   Confirmation is found in a passage of the fourth-century ecclesiastical historian, Eusebius, who in a reference to the end of Acts writes as follows:

'At that time, then, after making his defence, he [i.e. St. Paul] is said to have been sent again on the ministry of preaching, and, having entered the same city [i.e. Rome] a second time, to

---

[155] II Tim. 4.12.   [156] II Tim. 4.6,7.   [157] Philem. 22; Phil. 1.26; 2.24.
[158] II Tim. 1.6-4.5.   [159] e.g. II Tim. 1.6,8; 2.2,14; 3.14; 4.2.
[160] Tit. 1.5.   [161] Tit. 3.12.

have ended his life with martyrdom. While a prisoner in bonds he writes the Second Epistle to Timothy in which he mentions both his former defence and his imminent end. . . . This much we have said to show that the Apostle's martyrdom was not accomplished during that sojourn of his at Rome in which Luke wrote.'[162]

On this theory, known generally as 'the double imprisonment theory', it is conjectured that at the end of the 'two whole years' in Rome, at which point Acts stops short, St. Paul was tried, acquitted, and released: that he then undertook further missionary work, perhaps in Spain as he had previously intended,[163] but certainly in Macedonia,[164] Asia Minor,[165] and Crete;[166] and that he was then, for some reason unknown, re-arrested, taken back to Rome, re-tried, condemned, and executed. I Timothy and Titus are accordingly said to have been written from Macedonia while St. Paul was still at liberty; and II Timothy from Rome not long before his death.

This dating of the Epistles had obvious advantages over any attempt to find a place for them within the framework of the narrative of Acts. Acts tells us nothing about St. Paul's end; and there is, therefore, no compelling reason why we should assume that it followed immediately on the two years Roman captivity of Acts 28.30,31. After two years St. Paul may very well have been released: he may very well have embarked on another journey; and, if he made such a journey, his main concern may very well have been to make just the kind of provision for the future care and oversight of his churches that these Epistles reflect.

We must frankly recognize, however, that the direct evidence for St. Paul's 'double imprisonment' is very late, and consequently open to suspicion. Eusebius' statement, of course, may preserve a sound tradition, which, after being carefully handed down for generations, only first saw the light in written form in the early years of the fourth century. But far more probably it represents no more than the crystallization of an ingenious suggestion by some ancient scholar, which, originally put forward to explain the difficulties inherent in our Epistles in the light of the silence of Acts, soon found such general acceptance that it became eventually trans-

[162] Eusebius, *Hist. Eccl.*, 2.22.
[163] Rom. 15.24.
[164] I Tim. 1.3; Tit. 3.12; cp. Phil. 1.26; 2.24.
[165] I Tim. 1.3; II Tim. 4.13,20; cp. Philem. 22.
[166] Tit. 1.5.

formed into fact.   And if this be so, all so-called 'evidence' vanishes.   We remain in the realm of 'theory'.

But even if 'the double imprisonment theory' could be proved to be true, it would hardly affect the problem of the Pastoral Epistles in the form in which that problem presents itself to-day.   For the problem to-day is not primarily, Into what contexts in St. Paul's life should the Epistles be fitted?   It is rather, How much of them are genuine?   And it is only when we have answered this question satisfactorily that we can go on to fit whatever genuine parts we may be convinced that there are into their appropriate historical contexts, and also explain how the Epistles as they have come down to us came into being.

The evidence against the Epistles being genuine is overwhelming. In the first place, the entire atmosphere is that of an age later than St. Paul's : the stage of ecclesiastical organization depicted is later : the formalized 'pattern' of 'sound doctrine' inculcated is later; and the type of false teaching attacked is later.   Moreover, the writer's method of dealing with false teaching is certainly not that of St. Paul : St. Paul always meets false teaching by argument;[167] but here it is simply condemned.[168]   Important theological terms, too, have changed their meaning : thus, in genuine Pauline usage 'faith' always means a personal act of trust on the part of the individual believer,[169] but in the Pastorals it occurs frequently in the sense of a set of doctrinal propositions which the Christian must accept.[170]   Yet it is the linguistic argument that is really decisive : the number of words and phrases which are found in these Epistles (often more than once), but nowhere else in St. Paul, is very large indeed[171]—in fact, the general style is far nearer to the style of the ecclesiastical writers of the second century than it is to the style of St. Paul.

In spite, however, of the patently post-Pauline character of the Epistles as they stand there are here and there several indubitably Pauline phrases.[172]   Similarly, there are a number of personal details

[167] e.g. I Cor. 15.12-34; Gal. 3.1ff.; Col. 2.8-3.12.
[168] e.g. I Tim. 6.3.4; II Tim. 3.1-9; Tit. 3.10,11.
[169] e.g. Rom. 4.9; Col. 2.5.
[170] e.g. I Tim. 4.6; II Tim. 3.8; Tit. 1.13.
[171] As instances may be cited : (1) the word translated 'sound', literally 'healthy', applied to teaching, etc. (9 times); (2) the phrase 'faithful is the saying' (5 times); and (3) the insertion of 'mercy' between 'grace' and 'peace' in the opening salutations.
[172] e.g. 'I have determined' (Tit. 3.12; cp. I Cor. 2.2 and II Cor. 2.1); 'to come shortly' (I Tim. 3.14 and II Tim. 4.9; cp. I Cor. 4.19).

which strike the reader as very odd if invented—for example, the request to Timothy, 'the cloak that I left at Troas with Carpus, bring when thou comest, and the books, especially the parchments',[173] bears on its face the hall-mark of genuineness.

Hence, the prevailing modern theory is that some considerable time after St. Paul's death, probably in the earlier years of the second century, an unknown writer drastically edited what survived of St. Paul's correspondence with Timothy and Titus, remodelling it throughout, in order to make it applicable to the very different conditions obtaining in the Church of his own day. A few supposed fragments of the original letters have been identified by some scholars and assigned to definite historical situations—thus, it is suggested that Tit. 3.12-15 is from a letter addressed to Titus from Macedonia and written in between II Cor. 10-13 and II Cor. 1-9, while II Tim. 4.9-12 is part of a letter to Timothy recalling him to Rome after his visit to Philippi referred to at Phil. 2.19,23. But it would be unprofitable to go into further detail. By and large this theory fits the facts. And we shall explain the publication of the Epistles in St. Paul's name as an intelligible expedient adopted by a zealous and devoted churchman of the second century as the best means of safeguarding the purity of the tradition inherited from St. Paul in an age when everything seemed threatened by new-fangled and strange innovations.

Hebrews

Although in our Bibles this Epistle is given the title of 'The Epistle of Paul the Apostle to the Hebrews' and it consequently comes up for consideration along with the other epistles ascribed to St. Paul, it is worth noting at the outset that the Epistle itself makes no mention either of St. Paul as the author or of 'the Hebrews' as the recipients. In this respect it differs markedly from all the other 'Pauline' letters. All the others, whether genuine or not, start with an opening salutation couched in some such terms as 'Paul, an apostle of Christ Jesus, unto the saints which are at ——; Grace to you and peace'. But in Hebrews there is no opening salutation. Nor elsewhere are either the writer or the readers named.

None the less, from internal evidence it is possible to infer not a little about the circumstances of writing. The Epistle was

---

[173] II Tim. 4.13.

obviously addressed to people who were in danger of losing faith and heart under the stress of persecution and disappointment.[174] They had made a good start, but, like the Thessalonians in similar circumstances, they were impatient.[175] They were not tempted, it seems, to deny any essential part of the Gospel as they had received it. Nor, apparently, were they infected by any particular brand of false teaching. Rather was it that the primitive Gospel, as it had been preached to them, was proving inadequate to meet their needs. It required expanding and developing, and, to some extent, supplementing. And this the writer of the Epistle clearly saw. He provides, therefore, a complete and systematic restatement of the Gospel in terms which his readers would not only understand and appreciate, but also find especially helpful in surmounting the peculiar difficulties by which they at the time were faced.

In the process of restatement, however, the tradition remains intact. Christ and His work are still as central; and the Old Testament is quoted, even more copiously, as a storehouse of compelling proof. The 'Hebrews', too, are assured, as always, that the present world-order will be dissolved: [176] that 'there remaineth . . . a certain fearful expectation of judgement',[177] when Christ 'shall appear a second time'[178] and give the faithful a 'great recompense of reward';[179] and 'the day' is not far off.[180] But such references to the well-known and primitive elements in the Gospel are for the most part incidental; and even then they are frequently re-interpreted—as when the 'great recompense of reward' is further defined as 'salvation'[181] or 'the saving of the soul'.[182] For the writer expressly disclaims any intention of 'laying again a foundation' and of confining himself to 'first principles': he desires to 'press on'.[183] So without in any way ignoring these well-known elements he yet allows them to sink unobtrusively into the background while he concentrates his readers' attention on the gradual unfolding of his own new exposition of the place of Christ in the divine scheme for man's salvation, and illustrates and proves it point by point by reference to the Old Testament.

The two opening chapters state the main thesis. Christ is God's unique agent, His 'Son', the culmination of His revelation,

---

[174] Heb. 5.11-6.12; 10.23-29; 12.3-13.
[175] Heb. 6.11,12; 10.36.   [176] Heb. 12.25-28.   [177] Heb. 10.26-31.
[178] Heb. 9.28.   [179] Heb. 10.35.   [180] Heb. 10.25.
[181] Heb. 9.28.   [182] Heb. 10.39.   [183] Heb. 6.1.

through whom the great act of reconciliation between God and man has been at last accomplished.[184]   The unique sonship of Christ and His superiority to all other agents of God, particularly to the angels, are next established from Old Testament proof-texts;[185] and they form the basis of a direct *a fortiori* appeal to the readers.   The 'Hebrews' are beginning to 'drift away' from 'the things that were heard'[186]—i.e. from the Gospel.   But let them consider.   The Old Testament provides several examples of warnings given through angels which 'proved steadfast', in that they resulted in the punishment of those who disregarded them: how much the more worthy of attention, then, is God's message through His Son, and how much the greater will be the peril of those who refuse to heed it?[187]   For the Gospel is not concerned with trivialities: it is nothing less than the proclamation of God's design for the 'salvation' of mankind; and it is, further, well authenticated.[188] Christ Himself, the author and ground of 'all things',[189] through whom the message first was brought,[190] is also 'the author of salvation'.[189] A condition of His mission was that in every possible way He should 'be made like unto his brethren'[191]—the men and women He came to save: like them in His assumption of human 'flesh and blood',[192] like them in His endurance of human 'suffering',[193] and like them in His experience of the bitterness of human 'death'.[194]   And because of this He can help us.[195]   His victory over death and the Devil means our victory too.[196]   His path 'unto glory' is ours as well, whence we derive the right also to be called God's 'sons'.[189]   He is our 'High Priest' by whose 'propitiation' we all are presented before the heavenly mercy-seat of God.[191]

The remainder of the Epistle is little more that an expansion of this thesis.   The section 3.1-4.13 treats of the superiority of Christ to Moses—God's agent to Israel of old in the giving of the Law; while the story of Moses itself is held to refer unmistakably to 'the rest' to which Christ should lead the way.   Similarly, the section 4.14-5.10 treats of the superiority of the High Priesthood exercised by Christ to the so-called 'Levitical' high priesthood established in Aaron and transmitted through his sons: Christ is, in the

[184] Heb. 1.1-3.
[185] Heb. 1.4-14.
[186] Heb. 2.1.
[187] Heb. 2.1-3.
[188] Heb. 2.3.
[189] Heb. 2.10.
[190] Heb. 2.3.
[191] Heb. 2.17.
[192] Heb. 2.14.
[193] Heb. 2.9,10.
[194] Heb. 2.9,14.
[195] Heb. 2.18.
[196] Heb. 2.14,15.

words of the psalms, 'a high priest for ever after the order of Melchizedek'.[197]

And then, after an interlude on the 'Hebrews'' condition,[198] the significance of Christ's Melchizedek-priesthood is explained by a piece of typical Rabbinic reasoning.[199] Melchizedek, according to Genesis 14, was priest-king of Salem (an ancient name for Jerusalem), to whom Abraham 'gave a tenth out of all the spoils' on his return from 'the slaughter of the kings'. It is to be accepted as a general principle in such transactions, the writer argues, that the lesser gives tithes to the greater and not *vice versa*. Therefore, Melchizedek is proved greater than Abraham. But not greater than Abraham only. For contained 'in the loins' of Abraham 'when Melchizedek met him' were all his descendants, especially his great grandson Levi, Aaron the first high priest, and the whole of the Levitical priesthood. Since, then, on the lines laid down, Melchizedek is a type of Christ and Melchizedek's priesthood a type of Christ's priesthood, Christ must be greater than any Levitical high priest and his priesthood superior to theirs.

The particular superiority of Christ's high-priesthood is held to lie in its finality and permanence as contrasted with the transitoriness and impermanence of the Levitical. Christ, like Melchizedek, 'abideth for ever' and 'hath his priesthood unchangeable'.[200] He has been appointed 'a Son, perfected for evermore'.[201] And this is an essential part of the fulfilment of the promise made through Jeremiah,[202] that in the future a New Covenant should replace the Old.[203] The imperfect nature of the Old Covenant, mediated through Moses, appears from the fact that the propitiatory rites of the Day of Atonement were repeated again and again, year after year: they could never, therefore, effectively take away sin, or 'make perfect them that draw nigh'.[204] But Christ, the 'mediator' of the New and 'better' Covenant,[205] has 'through his own blood entered in once for all into the holy place [i.e. the heaven itself]',[206] having obtained 'eternal redemption'.[207] And by that single, all-sufficient, sacrifice of Christ on the cross the Christian too is both 'sanctified' and 'perfected'.[208] A 'new and living way' into the presence of God has been opened up.[209] The

[197] Psalm 110.4.   [198] Heb. 5.11-6.20.   [199] Heb. 7.1-28.
[200] Heb. 7.24.   [201] Heb. 7.28.   [202] Jer. 31.31-34.
[203] Heb. 8.7-13.   [204] Heb. 9.25; 10.1,3,11.   [205] Heb. 8.6; 9.15.
[206] Heb. 9.24.   [207] Heb. 9.12.   [208] Heb. 10.10,14.
[209] Heb. 10.20.

sacrifices ordained in the Law have been rendered otiose.[210] And the Law itself is now seen in its true perspective as 'a shadow of the good things to come'.[211]

The 'Hebrews', in consequence, must show 'boldness to enter into the holy place by the blood of Jesus' and 'hold fast the confession of their hope', remembering not only their Christian obligations, but also the perils that await them if they fail.[212] They have need above all of patience.[213] Here, the examples set by Israel's worthies in the past should prove a source of perennial inspiration.[214] They must hold fast to the pattern of day-to-day behaviour they have been taught, and not be 'carried away by divers and strange teachings'.[215] And then, after what looks like a concluding doxology,[216] follows the only personal message in the whole Epistle:

'But I exhort you, brethren, bear with the word of exhortation: for I have written unto you in few words. Know ye that our brother Timothy hath been set at liberty; with whom, if he come shortly, I will see you. Salute all them that have the rule over you, and all the saints. They of Italy salute you. Grace be with you all. Amen.'[217]

The Epistle is thus an outstanding instance of 'practical theology'. By tradition it is ascribed to St. Paul. But this tradition is certainly wrong.

In the first place, tradition itself, in the early period, is far from unanimous. St. Clement of Rome (*circa* 95), the first writer to show knowledge of the Epistle, cites it as anonymous. Origen, the great Alexandrian biblical scholar, who flourished in the first half of the third century, after discussing the various possibilities canvassed in his own day, concludes his observations with the remark, 'But who in fact did write the Epistle, God knows.' And St. Augustine of Hippo in North Africa (*circa* 400), the most influential theologian that the Western Church ever produced, started in his earlier writings by quoting it as the work of St. Paul, then later confessed to

---

[210] Heb. 10.18.   [211] Heb. 10.1.   [212] Heb. 10.19-31.
[213] Heb. 10.32-39.   [214] Heb. 11.1-12.13.   [215] Heb. 12.14-13.19.
[216] Heb. 13.20,21.
[217] Heb. 13.22-25. Cp. also the words immediately preceding the doxology, 'And I exhort you the more exceedingly to do this, that I may be restored to you the sooner' (13.19).

F

doubts, and eventually adopted the practice of quoting it as anonymous. The testimony of Eusebius on the point, furthermore, is definite that in his day (*circa* 300) the Pauline authorship was widely challenged.[218]

Secondly, as has been noted already, the author makes no claim to be St. Paul. We may argue that the personal details at the end suggest St. Paul; and we may go on to argue that in all probability the Epistle originally had an opening salutation of the normal type, and that this has been either lost accidentally or deliberately cut out. Yet this can be no more than conjecture. As the Epistle stands, St. Paul's name does not appear.

But it is the internal evidence provided by the Epistle's contents that is decisive. Admittedly, so long as we confine ourselves to generalities, there is nothing, either in the leading ideas or in the argument, that St. Paul could not have written. When we probe more deeply, however, we are confronted by a number of significant divergencies. There is, for example, no reference to the characteristically Pauline idea of being 'in Christ'. Little is said of the work of the Holy Spirit, who is only referred to in passing, and then primarily as the inspirer of Scripture.[219] Words, too, are used in different senses: thus, the writer's view of 'faith' as 'the assurance of things hoped for, the proving of things not seen'[220] is far removed from St. Paul's view, and corresponds to what St. Paul means by 'hope'.[221] Add to this that St. Paul's style is rugged, the style of Hebrews rhetorical: that different formulas are used by each in introducing Old Testament quotations:[222] that Hebrews is rich in compound Greek particles which never occur in St. Paul;[223] and it becomes impossible to maintain that St. Paul was the author.

In spite of this, though, Hebrews is not so much contradictory to St. Paul as complementary. And it was doubtless this fact which led some early Christian writers to put forward what may be termed a 'composite' hypothesis, according to which St. Paul was the author in the sense that he laid down the general lines that the Epistle was to follow, but left it to someone else to do the actual

---

[218] Eusebius, *Hist. Eccl.*, 3.3,5.   [219] e.g. Heb. 2.4; 3.7.   [220] Heb. 11.1ff.
[221] Cp. especially Rom. 8.24,25.
[222] St. Paul's favourite phrase is 'it is written' (e.g. Rom. 1.17; I Cor. 1.19); but Hebrews always uses some part of the verb 'to say', either in the active with 'he' or 'the Holy Ghost' as subject (e.g. 1.7; 3.7), or in the impersonal passive, 'it is said' (e.g. 3.15).
[223] e.g. ἐάνπερ three times in Hebrews, but never in St. Paul, or elsewhere in the New Testament.

writing. The most popular name suggested in this connection was St. Luke's; and the suggestion has much to commend it, since stylistically Hebrews is closer to the Lukan writings than to any others in the New Testament. St. Clement of Rome was another suggestion. And some asserted that St. Paul adopted this expedient and deliberately suppressed any mention either of his name or of his apostolic office, because he thought the 'Hebrews' not strictly within his sphere and that they might be put off by an apparent claim to authority over them. The absence of an opening saluta-tion is explained accordingly as due to St. Paul's humility.

If we reject a 'composite' solution, and allow St. Paul no share in the Epistle at all, we are left with a whole host of possible authors whose claims have been urged with almost equal justification both in ancient and modern times. There is only space here to refer to a few. St. Barnabas, for instance, is said to be especially suitable : he had been at one time St. Paul's companion in travel and might therefore be thought to have absorbed a good many of St. Paul's ideas : he was himself a Levite[224] and would naturally be interested in the details of the Levitical system; and as the bearer of a surname meaning 'son of exhortation '[224] he might reasonably be suspected of having written a 'word of exhortation '—the phrase by which the writer describes his own Epistle.[225] The Alexandrian Jew Apollos is another likely candidate : he too moved in the Pauline circle,[226] and had 'watered' the plot which St. Paul had 'planted' at Corinth : [227] as a man ' mighty in the scriptures '[228] he is just the sort of person to have made such copious use of proof-texts from the Old Testament; while the typological style of argument, of which Hebrews is so full, was particularly characteristic of the Jews of Alexandria. But undoubtedly the most startling suggestion so far made is that the Epistle was written by the converted Jewess Priscilla : both she and her husband were ' fellow-workers ' with St. Paul : [229] Hebrews exhibits several traces of the feminine point of view—e.g. the reference to the ' women ' who ' received their dead by a resurrection ';[230] and, anyway, we should not exclude the possibility that we owe at least one of the New Testament writings to a ' sister ' rather than a ' brother '! Yet that such a possibility as this last can be seriously entertained only serves to indicate the

[224] Acts 4.36.   [225] Heb. 13.22.   [226] Acts 18.24; I Cor. 16.12; Tit. 3.13.
[227] I Cor. 3.6.   [228] Acts 18.24.
[229] Acts 18.2,18; Rom. 16.3; I Cor. 16.19; II Tim. 4.19.   [230] Heb. 11.35.

enormous area of the field of choice. To-day we are no nearer an agreed solution than was Origen in the third century. It is as true now as it was then that, 'Who in fact did write the Epistle, God only knows.'

And we are confronted by a similarly indeterminate situation when we go on to ask, To whom was the Epistle written? and, When?

Since there is neither opening salutation nor reference to the readers by name elsewhere we are left almost completely in the dark. There is, it is true, the traditional title 'to the Hebrews'. There are also two scraps of information to be gleaned from the concluding personal message—from the greeting 'they of Italy salute you'[231] we may deduce that the Epistle was written either from or to Italy, for otherwise Italians are unlikely to have been mentioned specially; and from the statement that 'our brother Timothy hath been set at liberty'[232] we may surmise that it was written during Timothy's lifetime. But that is all.

It has been customary to take the 'Hebrews' of the title in the sense of Jewish, as distinct from Gentile, Christians. And this leads naturally to the supposition that the Epistle was addressed from Italy (very probably from Rome) to the Jewish Christians of Palestine to encourage them to stand firm against the attacks of their non-Christian compatriots at the time of the Jewish War (66-70). Alternatively, it is suggested that it was addressed, not from, but to, Rome, where there was certainly a large body of Jewish Christians throughout the first century: that the 'chastening'[233] referred to was the persecution of Nero (64-65), which had already resulted in the deaths of St. Peter and St. Paul;[234] and that so is explained the noteworthy fact that it is in the Epistle of St. Clement of Rome that Hebrews is first quoted. Objections have been raised against both these views. It has been maintained, on the one hand, that if the Epistle were indeed addressed to Palestine at the time of the Jewish War we should expect more specific references to the political situation then existing. On the other hand, it has been argued that there is no evidence for supposing that the Jewish Christians at Rome were ever regarded as in any way a separate community. Even so, both views are eminently reasonable.

It is at this point that it is worth putting the question, To what extent can we rely on the traditional title? For we have no right

[231] Heb. 13.24.   [232] Heb. 13.23.   [233] Heb. 12.7.   [234] Heb. 13.7.

to assume either that it derived from the author, or that, if not, it is based on sound information. No normal letter-writer gives his letter a title. We are consequently justified in believing that all titles attached to letters in the New Testament are later additions, supplied by editors when the individual letters were collected together. When a letter began with an opening salutation, and also, as in some instances, named the readers subsequently,[235] the addition of a title was easy. But with Hebrews it was not easy. Here there was neither opening salutation nor mention of the readers by name anywhere. An editor was therefore thrown back upon inference from the contents. In other words, he was in exactly the same position as the modern student.

Seeing that so much of the Epistle consists of appeal to the Old Testament, the inference that the readers were 'Hebrews' is both intelligible and sensible. But that does not make it any less an inference or exalt it into the category of evidence. Nor, when we examine it closely, is it by any means entirely satisfactory even as an inference. Apart from the appeal to the Old Testament there is nothing in the Epistle to suggest a Jewish-Christian connection. There is in fact not a little to be said to the contrary. The Greek style throughout is excellent: the Old Testament quotations follow the 'Septuagint' version used in the Dispersion, and not the original Hebrew; while the total repudiation of Judaism as a religious system, and the description of the Law as no more than 'a shadow of the good things to come',[236] is hardly the sort of thing either to be put forward by a writer who professed the kind of Jewish Christianity that we hear about in the New Testament or to be well received by any known Jewish-Christian community. We have to remember that the Old Testament was in no way the exclusive possession of Jewish Christians: it belonged to all Christians equally; and appeal to it was universal. If, then, we insist that the readers of Hebrews must have been Jewish Christians merely because the author refers them time and time again to proof-texts from the Old Testament, we ought also to argue that because St. Paul does exactly the same when writing to the Romans, the Galatians, and the Corinthians, they, too, were Jewish Christians, although we are well aware that the majority of them were not.

Yet, if the traditional title be no more than the result of inference,

---

[235] e.g. II Cor. 6.11; Gal. 3.1.   [236] Heb. 10.1.

and that inference be insecure or mistaken, we are left with nothing more solid to go upon than the two scraps of information to be gleaned from the concluding personal message: (1) that the Epistle was written either from or to Italy, and (2) that it was written during Timothy's lifetime.

To sum up. All we can profitably say for certain is that the Epistle was written by an unknown author, to readers we cannot identify, some time between the sixth and ninth decades of the first century. It is in purpose a tract of encouragement, designed to help the readers to retain their faith and hope in days of severe trial and temptation to apostasy. And it effects its purpose by providing them with a much fuller and far richer interpretation of the Gospel than they had hitherto received.

Chapter Four

THE GOSPELS

IN THIS chapter an attempt will be made to show how the primitive oral Gospel of the earliest preachers was developed into the four written 'Gospels' as they are read in our Bibles to-day.

As we saw in our first chapter, the only difference between Christians and Jews to begin with was that whereas the Jews still looked forward to the fulfilment of God's promises in a vague and indefinite future and to the coming of a Messiah as yet unknown, the Christians asserted that the promises were already in process of fulfilment and that they knew who the Messiah was—the Jesus they had loved on earth. Christian preaching was in consequence primarily directed towards establishing the Messiahship of Jesus. And the main hinge on which the Christian argument turned was the alleged correspondence between the series of events connected with the life and death of Jesus and the series of events which the prophets of the Old Testament had foretold would herald the coming of 'the End'. If the preacher was to be successful it was therefore essential that he should not only be able to recount what were for him the supremely significant happenings in recent history, but also be prepared to interpret them in the light of the Old Testament scriptures, about the authority and truth of which both he and his audience were agreed.

The appeal to the Old Testament was thus fundamental to any convincing statement of the Christian case. The events connected with Jesus and the Old Testament prophecies explained one another, and it was the preacher's function to bring them together. Thus, St. Peter, on the day of Pentecost, explains the strange behaviour of himself and his friends, which had so scandalized many who witnessed it, by reference to the words of Joel about the outpouring of the Spirit 'in the last days': [1] and, conversely, it was only

[1] Acts 2.14-21.

when St. Philip had 'preached Jesus' to the Ethiopian that the latter could understand the true meaning of the passage in Isaiah, which up till then he had found so puzzling.[2] The events connected with Jesus and the prophecies of the Old Testament were by the preacher set side by side, their correspondence noted, and the inference drawn that the End was near and that Jesus was Messiah.[3] This is, of course, why the sermons recorded in Acts are so full of Old Testament quotations. The Old Testament was part of the Gospel; and a sound knowledge of its contents was a necessary element in the preacher's equipment.

But all preachers tend to repeat themselves; and if they are preaching to different people there is every reason why they should. Moreover, they often borrow ideas, and even phraseology, from other preachers they have heard and admired. It is improbable that the earliest preachers were exceptions in either of these respects. St. Paul, for example, is hardly likely to have preached a brand new sermon in each fresh synagogue he entered. Nor, again, is he likely to have been entirely uninfluenced by the preaching method of his predecessors. Indeed, his own words decisively negative any such possibility; for, when referring at a later date to the first sermons he delivered in Corinth, he affirms to the Corinthians:

'I make known unto you, brethren, the gospel which I preached unto you, which also ye received. . . . For I delivered unto you first of all that which also I received, how that Christ died for our sins according to the scriptures; and that he was buried; and that he hath been raised on the third day according to the scriptures.'[4]

This passage suggests a fairly well established and widely recognized tradition in preaching. And such a tradition there undoubtedly was—hence, we may surmise, the striking 'family likeness' between all the sermons in Acts, whether attributed to St. Peter, St. Paul, or anyone else.

We have to think, then, of a common body of traditional 'Gospel' material circulating freely in the primitive Church, consisting both of 'the things concerning Jesus'[5] and of appropriate proof-texts from the Old Testament. This material would be

---

[2] Acts 8.30-35.   [3] Cp. Acts 2.22-36; 17.1-3.   [4] I Cor. 15.1-4.
[5] Acts 18.25; 28.23,31; cp. Luke 24.19,27.

drawn upon by a preacher as circumstances demanded. Individual preachers, naturally, would have their particular interests and preferences, while individual audiences would want particular points expanded. But, if we may trust the available evidence, any radical departure from the traditional method was exceptional, as witness St. Paul's attempt at Athens to convince his critical enquirers by a more general philosophical approach.[6] This attempt was a failure;[7] and St. Paul left Athens for Corinth ' determined not to know anything . . . save Jesus Christ and him crucified '[8]—in other words, the Gospel as he had received it.

All this means that by constant repetition as it passed from mouth to mouth, not only the central Gospel proclamation, but also much of the traditional matter associated with it and by which its truth was demonstrated, came increasingly to assume a regular and stereotyped form. Some preachers would make notes to assist their memories: some of the audience, too, might occasionally jot down a *précis* of a whole sermon or a few odd points; and then others would borrow and copy these notes, no doubt rearranging them somewhat and adding from other sources. So, we must suppose, were compiled the first written collections of incidents from the life of Jesus, of sayings of His that had been treasured and handed down, and of proof-texts from the Old Testament. From these collections any subsequent preacher could choose at will—an incident to illustrate some special aspect of the Messiah's mission, a saying to settle a point in dispute, or a text from the Old Testament to prove that the event or situation with which he happened to be dealing was in accordance with what the Scriptures had foretold.

About the precise forms and dates of these collections we can do little more than guess. Probably, however, the need for written collections of Old Testament proof-texts would be felt first. Nowadays we can look up a passage with comparative ease: cheap printed Bibles are readily accessible; and the different books are all conveniently divided into chapters and verses. But it was not so in antiquity. Copies of the Scriptures were for private people difficult to obtain. Unless one was either very wealthy or very privileged one would normally have to go to the nearest synagogue to find the Scriptures complete. And even then the absence of any chapter or verse divisions made it hard to locate the passage required in a book of any length. Sometimes a passage might be said to occur

[6] Acts 17.22-31.   [7] Acts 17.32-34.   [8] I Cor. 2.2.

in a well-known ' section' which had been given a name—as when our Lord Himself refers to Exod. 3.6 as contained ' in the place concerning the Bush'.[9] But usually this was not possible. Anyone who wanted to quote had for the most part to be content with the more general ' in Isaiah the prophet',[10] or ' in the book of Psalms';[11] and when his memory failed completely he had no compunction in taking refuge in the much more indeterminate ' it is written',[12] or even ' one hath somewhere testified saying . . .'[13]

Yet in the circumstances of the early Christian mission a fair standard of accuracy in quotation was essential. The Jews, to whom the primary appeal was made, had as great a knowledge of their Scriptures as had the Christian preachers. They would inevitably be only too ready to challenge a preacher if he quoted a text inaccurately or ascribed it to a wrong source; and those who were not persuaded, and were concerned to defend their position, would no doubt be no less eager than were St. Paul's converts at Thessalonica to ' examine the scriptures daily ' to see' whether these things were so'.[14] The preacher, that is, had to be careful.

Few, if any, preachers would possess complete copies of the Scriptures of their own; and even if some were in possession of copies of certain books, there was a limit to the amount of luggage that could be carried on a preaching tour. A large number of valuable proof-texts could, of course, be committed to memory. But most preachers were probably more than willing to spare their memories by taking with them on their travels a handy collection of the more important texts they intended to use, which had been carefully copied from the Bible at home. This development had obvious advantages. Not only was the preacher freed from the necessity of choosing between the awkward alternatives of overburdening either his luggage or his memory, but he was also provided with the means of speedy access to any proof-text he might want. And in addition he was able to quote when occasion arose in a reasonably accurate form.

Apart from these considerations of inherent probability, the arguments for the existence and circulation of written collections of proof-texts in the primitive Church are three:

(1) We know that at a later date several such collections were in existence, the best known being St. Cyprian's *Testimonies* (*circa*

---

[9] Mark 12.26.   [10] e.g. Mark 1.2.   [11] e.g. Acts 1.20.
[12] e.g. Rom. 1.17.   [13] Heb. 2.6.   [14] Acts 17.11.

250). The general plan of works of this kind is always similar. The basis is a series of propositions, which, when taken together, cover either the whole field, or a selected area, of Christian teaching. As each proposition is brought forward it is supported by appropriate scriptural quotations. Thus, in the *Testimonies*, the proposition 'that Christ was to be born of the seed of David according to the flesh' is supported by quotations of several verses each from II Samuel, Isaiah, Psalms, St. Luke, and Revelation (all written out in full); while the next proposition 'that Christ should be born in Bethlehem' is supported by Micah 5.2 and Matt. 2.1,2. Since St. Cyprian was writing in the third century he quotes from the New Testament as well as from the Old. But although his is the oldest collection of proof-texts that has come down to us, there is no reason to suppose that he was himself entirely responsible for the contents, still less that he originated the fundamental idea. On the contrary, it is probable that in his *Testimonies* he was doing no more than adapt to the needs of his own generation a well-tried method of literary apologetic, which had already proved its value over and over again, and of which the origin is to be sought in the rudimentary collections of the primitive preachers, when the books of the Old Testament were the only scriptures to which the Christian appeal could be made.

(2) In the study of proof-texts in early Christian literature generally it has been observed that there is a tendency for different authors to associate the same texts together, that they frequently quote such associated texts in the same order, and that they sometimes agree in quoting a text with the same inaccuracy or (apparently) deliberate alteration. For instance, when quoting Isaiah 35.6 both St. Justin (*circa* 150)[15] and St. Irenaeus (*circa* 180)[16] add 'at his coming' at the beginning, although these words occur in no known manuscript or version of Isaiah: or, again, the two verses Isaiah 28.16 and 8.14 are similarly associated together and cited as prophetic of Israel's rejection of the Gospel both at Rom. 9.32,33 and I Pet. 2.6-8. It is, of course, always possible in such instances that one of the writers had read the other, or that the two knew one another, or that they had been pupils of the same master, or that the same associations or alterations occurred to both independently. But often enough the best explanation is that both drew their quotations from a common collection, in which the texts to be used to

[15] Justin, *Apol.*, 1.48.   [16] Irenaeus, *Adv. Haer.*, 4.33,11.

support a proposition had already been brought together, and, perhaps, subjected in the process to a few minor verbal alterations so that their 'testimony' to the proposition might the more easily be perceived.

(3) There are in St. Matthew a number of Old Testament quotations which are found in this Gospel only: they are usually introduced by some such phrase as 'that it might be fulfilled which was spoken by the prophet saying'; and in wording they agree neither with the Hebrew original, nor with the extant Greek translations, nor with any other version.[17] They form, in fact, a distinct group on their own—distinct, even, from the other quotations in the same Gospel. In so far as their wording is so peculiar and the introductory phrases lay such stress on the fulfilment of prophecy, it is probable that the evangelist abstracted them from a collection and used them as 'testimonies' to the truth of his own narrative as it moved from stage to stage.

The next class of Gospel material to be considered is the Words of Jesus. It is true that in the sermons recorded in Acts there is little specific reference to the Words of Jesus. But Jesus was certainly presented as Himself a preacher—hence St. Peter's appeal in the house of Cornelius to 'the word' which God 'sent unto the children of Israel, preaching good tidings of peace by Jesus Christ'.[18] Members of a preacher's audience were therefore bound to ask what Jesus had said: converts especially would be interested; and the evidence makes it clear that Christians everywhere valued and quoted His utterances as of unique importance and authority in all kinds of situations. Thus, St. Paul asks the Ephesian elders at Miletus to 'remember the words of the Lord Jesus . . .':[19] he assures the Thessalonians that his account of what will happen when the End at last arrives is in accordance with 'the word of the Lord';[20] and, when advising the Corinthians on the advantages of celibacy he is careful to distinguish between his own opinion (what 'I say')[21] and the Lord's explicit command ('not I, but the Lord').[22]

If we may judge from those that have been preserved in our Gospels, these Words of Jesus were of several types. There were, first of all, the simple pithy sayings, such as, 'He that is not with

[17] As examples may be quoted: Matt. 1.22,23; 12.17-21; 27.9,10.
[18] Acts 10.36.   [19] Acts 20.35.   [20] I Thess. 4.15.
[21] I Cor. 7.8,12.   [22] I Cor. 7.10,11.

me is against me, and he that gathereth not with me scattereth '[23]—
these, undoubtedly, were the most easily remembered and consequently the most often quoted : there were the similes, such as
the declaration to the disciples 'Ye are the light of the world': [24]
there were the extended similes, or as we call them 'parables', in
which the likeness of one thing to another is drawn out in some
detail, such as the Parable of the Mustard Seed : [25] there were stories
designed to drive home a particular religious truth, such as the unfortunately named 'Parable' of the Pharisee and the Publican;[26]
and there were also lengthy discourses on such outstanding topics
as what would happen in the times of the End.[27]

The fact that in our Gospels as they stand not a few of the Words
of Jesus frequently assume more than one outward form[28] should be
sufficient to call our attention to the complexity of the history of
their tradition. And the further fact that St. Paul could ask the
Ephesian elders to 'remember' (as if it was already well known)
a saying that finds no place in our Gospels should remind us that
the tradition was obviously at one time far fuller than that part of
it which has been preserved. The tradition, of course, derived
originally from the Lord's immediate followers. No doubt all
recipients were as careful as they could be to transmit it as they
had received it. But the human memory is fallible, and allowance
must be made for individual idiosyncrasies. So long as the tradition
remained unwritten there was inevitably considerable variation.
Some Words would be well known in one church and totally
unknown in another. Of the Words that were current in a number
of churches there would be several different versions. Some Words
would be forgotten and so disappear entirely. While occasionally
others, which to start with had nothing to do with Jesus at all,
would get swept into the general stream, to be treasured with the
rest and quoted as equally genuine and equally authoritative.

To-day no written collection has survived complete. A single
leaf, however, slightly mutilated, which must at one time have
formed part of a book of sayings, was discovered at Oxyrhynchus

[23] Matt. 12.30; Luke 11.23.   [24] Matt. 5.14.   [25] Mark 4.30-32.
[26] Luke 18.9-14.   [27] Mark 13.5-37.
[28] e.g. : The saying ' He that is not with me . . .' is preserved in identical words at
Matt. 12.30 and Luke 11.23, but in a somewhat different form at Mark 9.40: the
version of the Parable of the Mustard Seed given at Mark 4.30-32 agrees generally
with the version given at Luke 13.18,19, but differs in detail; and there are a number
of very marked divergencies between the versions of the discourse about the End
given at Matt. 24.4-51, Mark 13.5-37, and Luke 21.8-36.

in Egypt in 1897. It contains eight sayings in all, six of which are easily legible. Each one of them is preceded by the introductory formula, ' Jesus saith '; and as a group they provide an interesting commentary upon the state of the tradition at the time when the collection was put together and in the area from which it came.

The end of the first saying (only the end has been preserved) agrees exactly with the Lukan version of the saying about the mote and the beam—' and then shalt thou see clearly to cast out the mote that is in thy brother's eye '.[29] The sixth and seventh are variant versions of two other Gospel sayings—' A prophet is not acceptable in his own country, neither doth a physician work cures upon them that know him,'[30] and ' A city built upon the top of a hill and stablished can neither fall nor be hid.'[31] The fifth offers a partial parallel to Matt. 18.20—' Wherever there are [. . .] and there is one [. . .] alone, I am with him. Raise the stone and there shalt thou find me, cleave the wood and there I am.' While the second and third are (to us) entirely new—' Except ye fast to the world ye shall in no wise find the kingdom of God, and except ye keep the Sabbath ye shall not see the Father ', and ' I stood in the midst of the world, and in the flesh was I seen of them, and I found all men drunken, and none found I athirst among them, and my soul groaneth over the sons of men because they are blind in their heart.'

This fragment was found in Egypt, and it is to be dated about 200. But this really tells us little. The book of which at one time it formed a part may well have been a copy, perhaps even a copy of the third or fourth generation; and the collection it contained may well, therefore, have been put together somewhere else than in Egypt, and at any time during the previous hundred or hundred and fifty years. From the fragment itself we can infer nothing about either the place of origin or the date of the collection: we can only use it as a convenient illustration of what a typical collection was like.

For proof that written collections of the Words of Jesus did in fact exist in the early period we are thrown back upon the evidence of the Gospels.

Several times in the Gospels little groups of sayings occur which can hardly have been uttered together, since their subject-matter is

---

[29] Luke 6.42.
[30] Cp. Matt. 13.57; Mark 6.4; Luke 4.24; John 4.44.
[31] Cp. Matt. 5.14.

so obviously unrelated. It is difficult, for instance, to imagine Jesus saying to the Pharisees on one and the same occasion (as St. Luke represents Him as saying):

'Ye are they that justify yourselves in the sight of men; but God knoweth your hearts: for that which is exalted among men is an abomination in the sight of God. The law and the prophets were until John: from that time the gospel of the kingdom of God is preached, and every man entereth violently into it. But it is easier for heaven and earth to pass away, than for one tittle of the law to fall. Every one that putteth away his wife, and marrieth another, committeth adultery: and he that marrieth one that is put away from a husband committeth adultery.'[32]

and then following it immediately with the story of the Rich Man and Lazarus. The suspicion is aroused that we are dealing here with a group of originally separate sayings which the evangelist has put together merely because they came to him together. And this suspicion is confirmed by the observation that three of the sayings are also recorded by St. Matthew, but each in a different context,[33] and each, moreover, in a context different from that in which St. Luke has placed them all. Naturally, we cannot be certain that this group did not reach St. Luke by word of mouth. But his reference in his preface to the 'many who have taken in hand to draw up a narrative concerning those matters which have been fulfilled among us' puts it beyond doubt that he knew of a number of written documents. It is, therefore, more than likely that he derived this group, not from a circulating oral tradition, but from a written documentary source—i.e. from an early collection of sayings similar to that of which a fragment has been recovered from the sands of Oxyrhynchus.

And a detailed comparative study of the Words of Jesus throughout St. Matthew and St. Luke establishes the existence of such a collection on reasonably solid grounds. These Gospels share in common a considerable amount of material which is contained in neither St. Mark nor St. John; and it consists mainly of Words of Jesus. Sometimes the two versions are so dissimilar in detail that all that can be said to be common is the basic subject-matter:[34] in

[32] Luke 16.15-18. [33] Matt. 11.12,13; 5.18; 5.32.
[34] e.g. Matt. 25.14-30; Luke 19.12-27.

these cases it may legitimately be argued that the material reached the evangelists through independent channels and that there is no possible way of determining whether, when it reached them, it was in written form or not. But sometimes (and more often) the verbal parallelism is so exact as imperatively to demand the conclusion that both evangelists were using a common written source. Take for example:

Matt. 11.25-30	Luke 10.17-24
	And the seventy returned with joy, saying, Lord, even the devils are subject unto us in thy name. And he said unto them, I beheld Satan fallen as lightning from heaven. Behold, I have given you authority to tread upon serpents and scorpions, and over all the power of the enemy: and nothing shall in any wise hurt you. Howbeit in this rejoice not, that the spirits are subject unto you; but rejoice that your names are written in heaven.
At that season Jesus answered	In that same hour he rejoiced in the Holy Spirit,
and said, I thank thee,	and said, I thank thee,
O Father, Lord of heaven and earth, that thou didst hide these things from the wise and understanding, and didst reveal them unto babes: yea, Father, for so it was well-pleasing in thy sight. All things have been delivered unto me of my Father: and no one knoweth the Son, save the Father; neither doth any know the Father, save the Son,	O Father, Lord of heaven and earth, that thou didst hide these things from the wise and understanding, and didst reveal them unto babes: yea, Father; for so it was well-pleasing in thy sight. All things have been delivered unto me of my Father: and no one knoweth who the Son is, save the Father; and who the Father is, save the Son,

and he to whomsoever the Son
willeth to reveal him. Come
unto me, all ye that labour
and are heavy laden, and I will
give you rest. Take my yoke
upon you, and learn of me; for
I am meek and lowly in heart :
and ye shall find rest unto
your souls. For my yoke is
easy, and my burden is light.

and he to whomsoever the Son
willeth to reveal him.

[cp. 13.16,17]

And turning to the disciples,
he said privately, Blessed are
the eyes which see the things
that ye see : for I say unto you,
that many prophets and kings
desired to see the things which
ye see, and saw them not; and to
hear the things which ye hear,
and heard them not.

The special problem here is one of similarity in the midst of diversity. The Matthaean passage immediately follows a discourse delivered by Jesus on the occasion of an embassy from John the Baptist during the ministry in Galilee: the Lukan passage is an account of what took place when the Seventy reported to Jesus the success of their preaching mission during His last journey to Jerusalem. The final words in St. Matthew have no parallel anywhere in St. Luke; and conversely, the opening words in St. Luke have no parallel in St. Matthew. There is, however, a fairly close parallel between the final words in St. Luke and some words said in St. Matthew to have been addressed by Jesus to His disciples in Galilee when they came to Him and asked 'Why speakest thou in parables? '; while the central words in both passages (the prayer of thanksgiving) are almost verbally the same. So exact is the parallelism between the two versions of the prayer that they must have been derived from a common written source. Yet, if so, the dependence at this point must have been limited to the words of the prayer alone, for otherwise why should the evangelists place it in entirely different contexts, associate it with entirely different sayings, and introduce it with entirely different formulae? In

G

other words, the common written source from which the prayer of thanksgiving was drawn must have been something very like the Oxyrhynchus book—i.e. a collection of separate sayings with no contexts or 'settings' given, and with the simplest of introductions.

How far this argument is capable of extension it is difficult to say. Many scholars would assign the whole of the material shared in common by St. Matthew and St. Luke to a single written source, which they designate by the symbol 'Q'.[35] Some have gone further, and, on the basis of the internal evidence, have suggested a place of origin (e.g. Jerusalem or Antioch) and an approximate date (usually 50-60). In this case the variations between the two versions in our Gospels, however wide, are accounted for by supposing that both evangelists have edited, often drastically, the material as it came to them.

But, as we have seen already, by no means all of the common material can be assigned with equal confidence to a written (as distinct from an oral) source—the variations between the versions are sometimes very wide. Moreover, since some of it consists of parables as well as sayings,[36] and sayings of John the Baptist as well as sayings of Jesus,[37] if it was drawn from a single source, that source must have been considerably more than just a plain collection of separate sayings of the Oxyrhynchus type. Consequently, an increasing number of scholars to-day are coming to regard the solution of a single, written, 'Q' as an over-simplification. A very great deal of the common material unquestionably did reach the evangelists in written, documentary, form. Yet this need not mean, either that they were dependent exclusively on documents, or that, when they were dependent on documents, they were dependent on only one. We must envisage the situation as it was. The Words of Jesus were being handed on by word of mouth: they were also being written down; and there is no justification whatever for supposing that no two lines of oral tradition ever agreed in including, for example, the same parable, or that the same saying never found a place in two different written collections. In all probability, therefore, the common material reached the evangelists in several different ways. Some will have come independently by word of mouth. Some, also independently, in written collections. And some, indubitably, in one or more collections that were jointly used by both.

---

[35] Usually explained as the first letter of the German *Quelle* (=source).
[36] e.g. Matt. 13.33; Luke 13.20,21.   [37] e.g. Matt. 3.7-10; Luke 3.7-9.

Whether there be one 'Q' or several, though, is for our present purpose of small importance. However it be interpreted, the evidence of the material common to St. Matthew and St. Luke points unmistakably in the direction of there being in existence and general circulation at least one written collection of Words of Jesus, either during, or shortly after, the lifetime of St. Paul.

But the primitive preacher needed not merely a fund of Old Testament proof-texts and a store of Words of Jesus. He needed also to be well informed about the Acts of Jesus. For, if he was to prove his case, he had to parallel the Old Testament proof-texts, and support the Words of Jesus, by appropriate illustrations from His Acts—i.e. from the 'mighty works and wonders and signs which God did by him in the midst of you'.[38]

The most significant of these 'mighty works' was the Crucifixion-Resurrection sequence, by which were most clearly demonstrated at one and the same time God's disapproval of the Jewish verdict on Jesus, and Jesus' own unique status as Messiah.[39] This explains why so much space in our Gospels is devoted to this sequence: why in St. Mark, for example, the narrative of the events of the final week occupies no less than six chapters out of a total of sixteen; and why, furthermore, the only two explicit references to the Acts of Jesus in St. Paul's letters are both concerned with this period.[40]

Yet the 'mighty works' were not limited to the Crucifixion-Resurrection sequence. Jesus was preached as one who 'went about doing good, and healing all those that were oppressed of the devil'.[41] A preacher, accordingly, would have to be ready with examples. He would tell how Jesus healed a leper in Galilee,[42] or how he restored a blind man's sight at Jericho on his last journey to Jerusalem.[43] Converts, too, would ask for more detailed information about Jesus, and might be given an account of such an incident as the Transfiguration.[44] They might enquire what His attitude had been on such a controversial point as the observance of the Jewish Sabbath, and be told the story of how once He had been challenged by the Pharisees for allowing His disciples to pluck ears of corn and thresh them on the Sabbath, and how He rounded on

---

[38] Acts 2.22.
[39] Cp. e.g. Acts 2.23,24; I Cor. 1.23; 15.3,4.
[40] I Cor. 11.23,24; 15.3-7.
[41] Acts 10.38.
[42] Matt. 8.1-4; Mark 1.40-45; Luke 5.12-26.
[43] Matt. 20.29-34; Mark 10.46-52; Luke 18.35-43.
[44] Matt. 17.1-8; Mark 9.2-8; Luke 9.28-36.

them and finished by curtly informing them that 'the sabbath
was made for man and not man for the sabbath'.[45]   And everything would be associated with Old Testament parallels and
represented as the fulfilment of such a prophetic utterance as:

> 'The Spirit of the Lord is upon me, because he anointed me
>   to preach good tidings to the poor:
> He hath sent me to proclaim release to the captives, and
>   recovering of sight to the blind,
> To set at liberty them that are bruised, to proclaim the
>   acceptable year of the Lord.'[46]

Whether or not we are justified in supposing that there ever were
written collections of the Acts of Jesus, as distinct from written
Gospels, it is impossible to say.   Obviously, there was less need
for written Acts than for written Words or Old Testament proof-
texts.   An isolated text or a detached saying is by no means easy
to recall at will; and in both cases it is of some importance that they
should be quoted accurately.   But a story is remembered more
easily, especially if it leads up (as most of the Gospel stories do) to a
noteworthy or suggestive 'point'; and provided the 'point' is made
the precise wording of the story as a whole is of relatively little
significance.   Some scholars, however, have maintained that the
Crucifixion-Resurrection sequence assumed written form quite soon.
It has also been maintained that before our present Gospels were
written there were in circulation a number of written story-collec-
tions, in which the stories themselves were arranged, not in their
true chronological order, but according to their theme—thus, the
five stories in Mark 2.1-3.6 are said to reflect this type of arrange-
ment, the theme in this instance being 'conflict between Jesus and
the Pharisees'.

Probably there were at least a few such collections.   But about
their nature, as about their existence, we can only conjecture.   The
first embodiment of the Acts of Jesus in written form of which we
have any certain knowledge is The Gospel according to St. Mark;
though here, since the book is a 'Gospel' proper and not merely
a collection of Gospel material, a selection of the Words of Jesus
is included also,[47] and references are made throughout to the fulfilment of the prophecies of the Old Testament.[48]

[45] Matt. 12.1-8; Mark 2.23-28; Luke 6.1-5.   [46] Luke 4.18,19; from Isa. 61.1,2.
[47] e.g. Mark 4.1-34.   [48] e.g. Mark 1.2,3; 14.27.

St. Mark

It can be seen at once how closely St. Mark follows the scheme of the preacher's proclamation. In the house of Cornelius St. Peter is said to have traced the origin of the 'good tidings' of the Gospel to 'the baptism which John preached': [49] St. Mark appropriately begins with an account of John, who 'baptized in the wilderness and preached the baptism of repentance unto remission of sins'.[50] Next, St. Peter introduces 'Jesus of Nazareth, whom God anointed with the Holy Ghost and with power': [51] St. Mark, similarly, proceeds immediately to tell how 'Jesus came from Nazareth of Galilee' to be 'baptized of John', and how He saw 'the Spirit as a dove descending upon him', and how He heard a voice declaring that He was truly Son of God.[52] As a consequence of this 'anointing', St. Peter declares, Jesus 'went about doing good and healing',[53] and adds that he himself and his companions were witnesses of what Jesus did 'both in the country of the Jews and in Jerusalem': [54] the main bulk of St. Mark is accordingly a description of this activity (in which St. Peter and his fellow-disciples play a prominent part), leading up to the last journey to Jerusalem and the events of the final week.[55] The Jews then 'slew' Jesus, 'hanging him on a tree': [54] St. Mark gives details of how they did it.[56] But this was not the end. 'Him,' St. Peter concludes, 'God raised up the third day, and gave him to be made manifest, not to all the people, but unto witnesses . . . , even to us, who did eat and drink with him after he rose from the dead': [57] which, again, is a fitting summary of St. Mark's concluding chapter.[58]

What, therefore, the evangelist has done is to clothe a skeleton with flesh. His book is no biography in the modern sense of the

---

[49] Acts 10.37. [50] Mark 1.1-8. [51] Acts 10.38.
[52] Mark 1.9-11. [53] Acts 10.38. [54] Acts 10.39.
[55] Mark 1.12-13.2. [56] Mark 14 and 15. [57] Acts 10.40,41.
[58] It is extremely doubtful, however, if we have Mark 16 in the form in which it left the author's hand. Although verses 9-20 are found in the majority of manuscripts, the two oldest have nothing at all after the words 'for they were afraid' in verse 8, while other endings are found in other manuscripts. The most satisfactory explanation of these divergencies is that the Gospel circulated normally in the early Church in the form in which it appears in the oldest manuscripts (i.e. ending at 16.8): that this end was widely felt to be inadequate; and that several independent attempts were made to supply what was needed, one of which eventually gained general acceptance (i.e. 16.9-20). Whether the author himself actually ended his book at 16.8, or whether his original ending got lost accidentally through being torn off, it is impossible to say. But what is reasonably certain is that, if he did write anything after verse 8, what he wrote has not survived.

term: it is still essentially the 'Gospel' as the early preachers preached it—the proclamation of Jesus as Messiah.

John the Baptist's message is of the coming of a 'mightier'.[59] The 'mightier' comes in Jesus, whose Messianic office is attested by the voice of God.[60] No one else knows this except the demons.[61] But all the time Jesus acts as one with authority,[62] and scandalizes religious officialdom[63] by assuming the powers of the Messiah to forgive sins,[64] to dispense with fasts[65] and even the regulations concerning the Sabbath.[66] Once again His 'mighty works' compel the demons to recognize Him; but they are immediately silenced.[67] His fame, however, grows.[68] He then questions His disciples Himself; and St. Peter confesses Him as Messiah, only to be charged, as were the demons, to keep the knowledge secret.[69] The experience on the Mount of Transfiguration confirms St. Peter's insight:[70] but still silence is enjoined.[71] Jesus leads His disciples on, a distinct and lonely figure, beyond their comprehension.[72] By the mode of His triumphal entry,[73] and by the cleansing of the Temple,[74] He fulfills two Messianic prophecies.[75] And then, at last, before the High Priest He admits in the words of Daniel that He is indeed Messiah, and is at once condemned.[76] Yet God had set His seal on Jesus' mission. The women at the tomb are assured that He had risen.[77] He would surely come again, this time in glory 'on the clouds of heaven'.[78] And in the light of this assurance the Crucifixion is no tragedy: it is the means that God has chosen to show His triumphant power; and Jesus Himself had foretold that it would happen, and that 'on the third day' He would be raised, although the disciples, when He told them, had failed to understand.[79] Read in this way St. Mark is not what we mean by history. It is theology pure and simple.

From the first half of the second century St. Mark has been named as the author. Papias, bishop of Hierapolis about 140, is our earliest witness to this belief:

'Mark,' he writes, 'who had been the interpreter of Peter, wrote down accurately everything that he remembered, without,

[59] Mark 1.7. [60] Mark 1.9-11. [61] Mark 1.24.
[62] Mark 1.27. [63] Mark 2.7. [64] Mark 2.9.
[65] Mark 2.18-22. [66] Mark 2.23-27. [67] Mark 3.11,12.
[68] Mark 7.36,37. [69] Mark 8.27-30. [70] Mark 9.2-8.
[71] Mark 9.9. [72] Mark 10.32. [73] Mark 11.1-10.
[74] Mark 11.15-18. [75] Zech. 9.9; Mal. 3.1. [76] Mark 14.60-64.
[77] Mark 16.6. [78] Mark 13.26; 14.62. [79] Mark 8.31-33; 9.30-32; 10.32-34.

however, recording in order what was either said or done by
the Lord. For neither did he hear the Lord, nor did he follow
him, but afterwards, as I said, attended Peter, who adapted his
instruction to the needs of his hearers.'[80]

Papias did not make this statement off his own bat. He says that
he derived it from ' the Elder ', whom he obviously revered. It has,
therefore, a respectable ancestry. Moreover, it is inherently probable. John Mark of Jerusalem was a comparatively minor figure
among the leaders of the early Church, and it is unlikely that a
Gospel would ever have been ascribed to him unless there was some
valid reason for doing so. He is associated with St. Peter twice in
the New Testament, once in Acts,[81] and once in I Peter.[82] If, then,
he did ' follow' St. Peter on his travels as his ' interpreter', he may
very well have written down his preaching; and it is significant in
this connection that it is to one of St. Peter's sermons, as recorded in
Acts, that the skeleton of St. Mark so closely conforms.[83] Further,
there are, scattered throughout the Gospel, several rather curious
incidents and details,[84] which have no particular point in themselves,
but which are easily explicable if we suppose that St. Mark has
preserved St. Peter's own personal reminiscences.

   Some would deny outright this association of the evangelist with
St. Peter. They point to what they call a ' lack of cohesion' in
the narrative, and maintain that such an assortment of unrelated
oddments as makes up the body of the Gospel can hardly have been
derived directly from one of the chief participants. In addition,
they allege that the Gospel betrays an ' anti-Petrine' tendency—
i.e. that St. Peter is often rebuked by Jesus,[85] that he is frequently
represented in an extremely unfavourable light,[86] and that in the
end he denies his Master;[87] all of which is said to argue decisively
against any close contact with St. Peter. We have to remember,
however, that Papias distinctly states that St. Mark did not write
' in order '; and also he implies that he wrote after St. Peter's death,
when his former failures had been amply atoned for by his subsequent missionary labours and the glory of a martyr's crown. In

[80] Quoted by Eusebius, *Hist. Eccl.,* 3.39,15.
[81] Acts 12.12.   [82] I Pet. 5.13.   [83] See above, p. 101.
[84] e.g. Mark 1.35-39; the Aramaic words *talitha cumi* at v. 41, said to have been
spoken when only St. Peter and two others were present; or the mention of ' green
grass ' at 6.39.
[85] e.g. Mark 8.33.   [86] e.g. Mark 9.5,6.   [87] Mark 14.66-72.

this case, St. Mark will in effect be saying 'See how the Risen Christ can take even the feeblest of human clay, mould it, strengthen it, and use it in His service.'

Tradition affirms that St. Peter preached finally in Rome, and that he was martyred there in the persecution that broke out under the Emperor Nero in 64. St. Mark's presence in Rome about this time is independently attested by St. Paul, who mentions him as sending greetings in Colossians[88] and Philemon[89]—that is, if we agree in assigning these Epistles to the period of the Roman captivity. And it may be that it was during this period, when St. Peter was still alive, that St. Mark wrote down his preaching.

But, as we have seen, the statement of Papias implies that St. Mark wrote after St. Peter's death; and the portrait of St. Peter in the Gospel reflects the recollection of his martyrdom. The representation, too, of the Lord's last journey to Jerusalem as a 'road of sorrows',[90] with the accompanying emphasis on suffering as exemplified in such sayings as, 'If any man would come after me, let him deny himself and take up his cross and follow me',[91] suggests that the writer was addressing a martyr church. From the note at 7.3,4 it is clear that he was writing for readers unfamiliar with the customs of Palestinian Jewry. He uses also here and there a Latin word or phrase.[92]

Hence, everything points to Rome as the place of origin of the Gospel. We may accept St. Mark as its author. And we may best date it shortly after the Neronian persecution—say in 66.

St. Matthew

St. Matthew is an enlarged edition of St. Mark.

It has been recognized for centuries that there is the closest possible literary connection between the two. But until just over a hundred years ago it was usually supposed that it was St. Mark who had 'abbreviated' St. Matthew. This was because St. Matthew is obviously by far the longer; and also because, inasmuch as St. Matthew was popularly attributed to one of the Lord's disciples, it was argued that it must necessarily be given precedence over such a 'second-hand' work as St. Mark—an argument which was easily convertible by popular assumption into the idea that it was also prior in time.

[88] Col. 4.10.   [89] Philem, 24.   [90] Mark 8.31-10.45.   [91] Mark 8.34.
[92] e.g. *speculator* for a soldier of Herod's bodyguard at 6.27.

A detailed examination of the two side by side, however, makes it clear that so far from St. Mark being an 'abbreviation' of St. Matthew, the truth is the other way about. We may cite as a specimen passage:

Matt. 8.16,17	Mark 1.32-34
And when even was come, they brought unto him	And at even, when the sun did set, they brought unto him all that were sick, and them that were possessed with devils.
many possessed with devils: and he cast out the spirits with a word,	
and healed all that were sick:	And all the city was gathered together at the door. And he healed many that were sick with divers diseases, and cast out many devils; and he suffered not the devils to speak, because they knew him.
that it might be fulfilled which was spoken by Isaiah the prophet, saying, Himself took our infirmities, and bare our diseases.	

It will be seen at once that there are fewer words in the first column than in the second, although the same incident is recorded in both. There is no mention in St. Matthew of St. Mark's 'when the sun did set', of 'all the city' being 'gathered together at the door', of the different kinds of diseases, or of the devils' attempts to speak. On the other hand, there is the statement in St. Matthew that the cures were the fulfilment of a prophecy in Isaiah, a statement absent from St. Mark.

It is, of course, theoretically possible that St. Mark knew the Matthaean version: that he deliberately ignored the reference to Isaiah; and that he then (like a modern preacher) proceeded to tell the same story at greater length. Possible, but hardly probable. Rather is it likely that the Markan version is the earlier: that the author of the Matthaean condensed it by omitting such an unnecessary duplicate expression as 'when the sun did set', or such an unessential eye-witness touch as 'and all the city was gathered together at the door'; and that he devoted the space so saved to underlining the Lord's Messianic office by adding an Old Testament proof-text.

Similar observations may be made about other parallel passages, and extended to cover the relationship between the two Gospels as a whole. Over ninety per cent of the material in St. Mark appears also in St. Matthew, almost always in the same order, but in a condensed form and interspersed with other material not found in St. Mark (e.g. The Sermon on the Mount). It is eminently reasonable to maintain that the author of St. Matthew condensed St. Mark, and added from such other sources as were available to him: it is not reasonable to maintain that St. Mark 'abbreviated' St. Matthew by omitting such an outstanding item as the Sermon, and yet at the same time expanded what he retained by writing it out at greater length. Add that St. Mark's narrative is throughout more graphic: that his Greek style is less polished:[93] that he alone several times preserves the Lord's words in the original Aramaic;[94] and there can be no doubt whatever that his Gospel is the earlier.

Thus, just as St. Mark took the skeleton of the primitive oral Gospel and clothed it, as we have seen, with flesh, so the later evangelist treated St. Mark. He added material from a document or documents used also in St. Luke.[95] And he incorporated much as well that is peculiar to himself. This last material consists partly of Words of Jesus,[96] partly of Acts of Jesus,[97] and partly of minor incidents that fill out the Markan narrative.[98]

From these additions, and even more from the way he has sometimes altered the wording in St. Mark, we can infer not a little about his interests and general outlook. He is at pains to make things plain, as when at 17.13 he adds to St. Mark, 'Then understood the disciples that he spake unto them of John the Baptist.' He stresses the doctrine of the Divine Fatherhood (God is referred to as 'Father' only four times in St. Mark, but forty-two times in St. Matthew). He is anxious that no one shall be in doubt who Jesus really was: in St. Mark St. Peter confesses simply 'Thou art the Christ',[99] but in St. Matthew 'Thou art the Christ, the

---

[93] Thus, the 'bed' on which the paralytic lay is in Mark 2.1-12 a *krabbaton* (said by the Greek grammarians to be a vulgar word); in Matt. 9.1-8 it is the normal *kleine*.

[94] Mark 5.41; 7.11,34; 14.36.

[95] See above, pp. 95ff.

[96] e.g. Matt. 13.36-52.

[97] e.g. Matt. 17.24-27.

[98] e.g. Matt. 27.24,25.

[99] Mark 8.29.

Son of the living God '.[100]   And he is interested especially in the
details of the End; for not only does he follow up St. Mark's great
End-time discourse[101] with a chapter and a half of further teaching
on the same theme,[102] but he frequently re-words St. Mark so as
to bring out the particular details that interested him, as the following comparison will show:

<table>
<tr><td>Matt. 16.27,28</td><td>Mark 8.38; 9.1</td></tr>
<tr><td>For</td><td>For whosoever shall be
ashamed of me and of my words
in this adulterous and sinful</td></tr>
<tr><td>the Son of man</td><td>generation, the Son of man
also shall be ashamed of him,</td></tr>
<tr><td>shall come in the glory
of his Father with his
angels; and then shall he
render unto every man accor-
ding to his deeds.</td><td>when he cometh in the glory
of his Father with the holy
angels.</td></tr>
<tr><td>Verily I say unto you,
There be some of them that
stand here, which shall in
no wise taste of death, till
they see the Son of man
coming in his kingdom.</td><td>And he said unto them,
Verily I say unto you,
There be some here of them
that stand by, which shall in
no wise taste of death, till
they see
the kingdom
of God come with power.</td></tr>
</table>

There is, too, throughout St. Matthew a strongly Jewish
flavour, which, although plainly Jewish-Christian, nevertheless
attests the evangelist's own Jewish background and connections.
Quotation from the Old Testament is more frequent, more pointed,
and more far-reaching in its effects, than in any other Gospel—
witness the picture of Jesus entering Jerusalem seated on two animals
instead of one (as in St. Mark),[103] merely because the prophecy of
Zechariah spoke of both ' an ass ' and ' a colt the foal of an ass '.[104]
There are a number of constantly recurring Rabbinic phrases, such
as ' doing the will '.[105]   The scribes and the Pharisees ' sit on Moses'

[100] Matt. 16.16.   [101] Mark 13.   [102] Matt. 24.37-25.46.
[103] Matt. 21.1-9; Mark 11.1-10.   [104] Zech. 9.9.   [105] Matt. 7.21; 12.50; 21.31.

seat', and men must 'do and observe' whatsoever they bid.[106] Jesus Himself is portrayed as the new lawgiver, who, like Moses of old, issues His commands from the Mount.[107] He came 'not to destroy the law or the prophets . . . but to fulfil'; and the relationship between the new and the old is immediately and minutely explained.[108] His earthly mission was limited to 'the lost sheep of the house of Israel';[109] and it is not until after the Resurrection that His disciples are commissioned to preach to 'all nations'.[110] The Christian Gospel, that is, has not (in St. Paul's phrase) 'made the Law of none effect': it has 'established' the Law by transcending it.[111]

And, finally, St. Matthew is the only Gospel in which the word 'Church' is mentioned and applied to the body of believers.[112] Here is proof, not merely of the evangelist's familiarity with the term, but also of his interest and concern for the corporate life of the Christian community.

Who he was, where he wrote, and when, it is impossible to say for certain.

All early writers who discuss the question assert that St. Matthew was the first of the Gospels to be written (according to St. Irenaeus it was written 'while Peter and Paul were founding the church at Rome'—i.e. *circa* 50-65); and they identify the evangelist with St. Matthew, one of the Twelve, who in this Gospel alone is described as 'Matthew the publican'[113] and equated with the publican Levi mentioned in St. Mark and St. Luke.[114] The majority state further that he wrote originally in Hebrew for the benefit of converted Jews, and that our Greek Gospel is a translation; and also that he wrote in Palestine.

The unsatisfactoriness of this view of the Gospel's origin will be immediately apparent in the light of the preceding discussion. If St. Matthew was based on St. Mark, of which it is a new and enlarged edition, it cannot have been the first of the Gospels to be written. The dependence on St. Mark further precludes the supposition that it is a translation of a Hebrew original; for St. Mark was known to the author of St. Matthew in Greek, as we can see from the pains he took to improve the style. Nor, again, is it conceivable that one of the Twelve, who had himself been present

---

[106] Matt. 23.2,3.　　[107] Matt. 5.1; 8.1.　　[108] Matt. 5.17-48.
[109] Matt. 10.5,6; 15.24.　[110] Matt. 28.19,20.　[111] Rom. 3.31.
[112] Matt. 16.18; 18.17.　[113] Matt. 10.3.　　[114] Matt. 9.9; Mark 2.14; Luke 5.27.

as a leading participant in so many of the situations that he describes, should have been thus dependent for his primary source on an account, which, however accurate, was admittedly second-hand. St. Matthew, manifestly, was not the author.

But this is not to say that St. Matthew had no connection with the Gospel. He may very well have been responsible for collecting some of the sayings which are so noteworthy a feature of the Gospel. He may have put together a collection of Old Testament proof-texts; and it was possibly from this collection that the author of the Gospel drew those quotations whose curious wording has already been noticed.[115] In some such way as this the association of St. Matthew's name with the Gospel may be satisfactorily explained. But for the author we must look elsewhere.

Most, nowadays, think of him as an unnamed writer of some local church, who revised St. Mark, adding such other material as was available and valued, in order to produce a Gospel as full, as succinct, and as well arranged as might be, for public reading in the church to which he belonged—that he was, in fact, himself a ' scribe who hath been made a disciple to the kingdom of heaven ' and ' like unto a man that is an householder, which bringeth forth out of his treasure things new and old '.[116]

Many guesses have been made about the identity of his church. Jerusalem, for instance, accords well with the Gospel's Jewish-Christian flavour; and it is also supported by the tradition of Palestinian origin. Yet that the Gospel was written in Greek, and was based on a Greek source, tells rather in favour of a cosmopolitan Jewish-Greek city, like Caesarea or Antioch. It is an early bishop of Antioch, St. Ignatius, who first shows definite knowledge of the Gospel; and if it had the authority of so important a Christian centre as Antioch behind it, its widespread dissemination and unchallenged position are easily accounted for. St. Ignatius was martyred about 110, and if St. Mark is rightly dated about 66, the composition of St. Matthew must lie between the two extremes.

Thus, the most likely solution is that the Gospel was written at Antioch between the years 70 and 100. But who the author was must remain an unsolved problem.

St. Luke

This Gospel, unlike the others, opens with an author's preface:

[115] See above, p. 92.   [116] Matt. 13.52.

'Forasmuch as many have taken in hand to draw up a narrative concerning those matters which have been fulfilled among
us, even as they delivered them unto us, which from the beginning
were eye-witnesses and ministers of the word, it seemed good to
me also, having traced the course of all things accurately from
the first, to write unto thee in order, most excellent Theophilus;
that thou mightest know the certainty concerning the things
wherein thou wast instructed.'[117]

We are reminded at once of similar prefaces in contemporary
pagan writers. A patron, Theophilus, is addressed by name: the
author declares his purpose: he emphasizes the pains he has been
at to ensure an accurate and orderly narrative; while his Greek
style at this point is so much more idiomatic and literary than
anything found elsewhere in the New Testament (or indeed in the
rest of his own work) that it seems as if he was making a deliberate
effort to catch the eye of the world of letters.

Unfortunately, the address to Theophilus tells us little. Some
think that Theophilus (which means 'beloved of God') was the
real name of a converted pagan of good social standing who had
commissioned the Gospel. Others think it a pseudonym employed
by the evangelist to conceal his patron's identity at a time when
the open profession of Christianity might involve penalties for those
in high places. Yet others that it is a generic name for any Christian, and that the evangelist meant no more by it than 'Christian
reader'. But be this as it may, both the style and the content of
the preface make us aware at the very beginning that 'the things
concerning Jesus' are being presented, not to any narrow circle of
half-educated Jews or Jewish-Christians, but to a wider and more
cultivated Gentile public, familiar with the conventions established
by the authors of Greece and Rome.

The reference to 'many who have taken in hand to draw up a
narrative concerning those matters which have been fulfilled among
us' makes it plain that the evangelist knew of others who had
attempted the same task before him. He does not say that he had
used their work: in fact, from the way he claims himself to have
'traced the course of all things accurately from the first' it may well
be maintained that he was purposely trying to create the impression
that he was working quite independently, and relying solely on the

[117] Luke 1.1-4.

most trustworthy oral tradition. But a comparison of his Gospel with St. Mark reveals that it stands in the same relationship to it as does St. Matthew—i.e. that it is another 'enlarged edition'.

The arguments for this conclusion are *mutatis mutandis* the same as those outlined above in the section on St. Matthew—namely, that the vast majority of the material contained in St. Mark is contained also in St. Luke, in very much the same order, and in often identical, but usually fewer, words:[118] yet St. Luke contains more material than does St. Mark: we must, therefore, decide that it was the author of St. Luke who was using St. Mark, and not St. Mark St. Luke. We should observe here, however, that in St. Luke the earlier Gospel is treated more freely than in St. Matthew: there are more omissions,[119] more re-arrangements,[120] and on the whole more minor alterations and interpretations.[121]

In addition to St. Mark the evangelist shared also with St. Matthew the document, or documents, known as Q.[122] Whether he used any other documents besides these is questionable. It is often maintained that the more important narrative sections peculiar to the Gospel (such as the birth-stories at the beginning) were drawn from a documentary source; and many would say the same of the characteristically Lukan parables (such as the Good Samaritan,[123] the Lost Son,[124] or the Pharisee and the Publican).[125] But the preface suggests that the author made careful enquiries and collected a fair proportion of his material by word of mouth. If so, there is no need to conjecture additional documentary sources. The considerable quantity of matter, which is found in this Gospel alone, is just as easily, and probably far more satisfactorily, accounted for as the evangelist's writing up of the results of his own enquiries.

As we saw when dealing with St. Matthew, an evangelist's interests and general outlook may be inferred partly from the way he treats his sources and partly from what he adds to them. What, then, may be inferred on the basis of these criteria about the interests and general outlook of the author of St. Luke?

The preface has already revealed that he was writing primarily

---

[118] Cp. e.g. Mark 4.1-5.43 and Luke 8.4-56.
[119] Thus, the whole section Mark 6.45-8.26 is omitted entirely.
[120] e.g. Mark 6.1-6 is transferred to Luke 4.16-30.
[121] Cp. e.g. Matt. 8.16,17; Mark 1.32-34; Luke 4.40,41.
[122] See above, pp. 95ff.   [123] Luke 10.25-37.
[124] Luke 15.11-32.   [125] Luke 18.9-14.

for Gentiles; and interest in the Gentile Mission is reflected in almost every page.   The aged Simeon in the Temple, with the infant Jesus in his arms, sings of the 'salvation' which God has 'prepared before the face of all peoples, a light for revelation to the Gentiles'.[126]   The quotation from Isaiah at Mark 1.3 is of one verse only, but at Luke 3.4-6 it is extended by two extra verses in order to end with the words 'And all flesh shall see the salvation of God'. The Seventy are sent out to preach[127]—proleptically, it seems, to the seventy nations of the world.   Again, when the evangelist comes to re-write St. Mark's 'End-time' discourse in chapter 21 of his own Gospel, he speaks of the destruction of Jerusalem as decreed by God 'until the times of the Gentiles be fulfilled'[128]— we are reminded of St. Paul's argument in Rom. 9-11, and of his formula 'a hardening in part hath befallen Israel until the fulness of the Gentiles be come in'.[129]   And it is in conformity with this guiding principle that the Lord's ministry is presented.   Historically that ministry was limited to Palestine and for the most part confined to Jews.   But the evangelist never tires of stressing the interest taken in the outcasts from official Judaism ('publicans', 'sinners', and 'Samaritans') and the encomiums pronounced upon them.[130] The Lord's mission, he is saying, was universal from the start: it was only circumstance that might make it appear that it was not.

No less than sixteen times in this Gospel Jesus is referred to in narrative as 'the Lord'.[131]   Since this usage is characteristic of St. Luke, being found neither in St. Mark nor St. Matthew, it is not fanciful to see here the influence of the ecclesiastical phraseology with which the author was familiar.   For Gentile Christians the central figure of the Gospel story, whatever He may have been on earth in Palestine, was the exalted Jesus of their worship, whom they had been enabled by the Spirit to confess as 'Lord' on their conversion,[132] and whom they referred to habitually as 'the Lord' in daily life.[133]   The evangelist, in consequence, slips naturally into the accustomed title.   It is interesting, too, to note how time and again he brings out the centrality of Jesus by representing Him more often than any other Gospel writer as surrounded by crowds or accompanied by disciples who function (in dramatic terms) as a kind of chorus.   Yet all the time Jesus Himself is pre-eminently

[126] Luke 2.30-32.
[128] Luke 21.23,24.
[130] e.g. Luke 7.36-50; 10.30-37; 19.1-10.
[132] Cp. I Cor. 12.3; 8.5.

[127] Luke 10.1-16.
[129] Rom. 11.25.
[131] e.g. Luke 7.13; 17.5,6; 22.61.
[133] Cp. I Cor. 9.14; 10.21.

distinct: for example, whereas Mark 14.26 is content to merge Jesus in his disciples ('And when they had sung an hymn, they went out into the mount of Olives'), Luke 22.39 makes the distinction clear-cut ('And he came out and went . . . unto the mount of Olives: and the disciples also followed him'). The point of view of the Christian believer of a later date is thus unconsciously read back into the details of the story.

Sometimes, as it were by anticipation, a pressing problem is answered. The early preachers, for instance, had proclaimed the imminence of 'the Day' and the Lord's speedy return on the clouds of heaven. But the years had gone by: 'the Day' had not dawned: neither had the Lord returned. The result was the despair of many. In this situation the evangelist has a message for the Church. It is not merely the previously mentioned consideration that 'the times of the Gentiles' must be 'fulfilled'.[134] The faint-hearted can fortify themselves from the very Words of Jesus. When asked on one occasion by the Pharisees 'when the kingdom of God cometh', Jesus Himself had warned them that 'the kingdom of God cometh not with observation'.[135] The Parable of the Pounds, moreover, which speaks of 'a nobleman' going 'into a far country to receive for himself a kingdom and to return', had been uttered precisely because there were some with the Lord at that moment who erroneously thought 'that the kingdom of God was immediately to appear'.[136] The anxious must therefore be patient and wait on God's good time. They need have no anxiety. 'Fear not, little flock,' the Lord had said, 'for it is your Father's good pleasure to give you the kingdom.'[137]

The final point that we may notice is the evangelist's attitude to the Twelve. In this Gospel only are they called 'apostles'.[138] The name is said to have been given when they were chosen.[139] Passages in St. Mark in which they appear in a discreditable light are either omitted,[140] or else palliated by the addition of an excuse—as when 'Peter and those with him' are said to have been 'heavy with sleep' on the Mount of Transfiguration and therefore not responsible for what they said,[141] or when in the Garden of Gethsemane they are represented as sleeping 'for sorrow'.[142] Here the evangelist's natural reverence for the Twelve obtrudes itself. For

[134] Luke 21.24. [135] Luke 17.20,21. [136] Luke 19.11ff. [137] Luke 12.32.
[138] Luke 6.13; 9.10; 17.5; 22.14; 24.10. [139] Luke 6.13.
[140] e.g. Mark 8.32,33; 10.35-45. [141] Luke 9.32. [142] Luke 22.45.

by the time he wrote his Gospel they were looked back upon (and up to) as the pillars of the Church.

With the unanimous ecclesiastical tradition that the evangelist was St. Luke there is no need to quarrel. St. Luke is mentioned only three times in St. Paul's letters,[143] and nowhere else in early Christian literature. His obscurity is accordingly the best possible argument for the soundness of the tradition. Further, if (as will appear when we come to Acts) he was one of St. Paul's companions in travel, the points of contact with St. Paul fall easily into place, as does also the unmistakably Gentile outlook that pervades his Gospel from end to end.

Tradition also says that he wrote in Greece. This may well be true. But we have no means of deciding either one way or the other.

Similarly, the date must be left open. In so far as St. Luke is an enlarged edition of St. Mark it must have been written after 66—if that date be accepted for St. Mark: in so far as it was apparently known to the author of St. John it must be earlier than whatever date be fixed for that Gospel.[144] The only internal indication is provided by certain alleged references to the fall of Jerusalem, which took place in 70.[145] In these passages, it is claimed, the evangelist re-writes the Words of Jesus to accord more closely with the details of what had already taken place when he was writing—the 'desolation'[146] of Jerusalem was a fact, the city had indeed been 'trodden down of the Gentiles',[147] and 'wrath'[148] poured out on the Jews. But in any case his Gospel is redolent of the fears and aspirations of the second generation of Christians rather than the first. A date between 80 and 90 is as near as we are likely to get.

St. John

No one who turns to St. John from St. Matthew, St. Mark, and St. Luke, can fail to be struck by the many differences between this Gospel and its predecessors. To say this is not to suggest that there are no differences between the first three Gospels—there obviously are, and the more significant have already been discussed. It is, however, to point out that the differences between any two of them are rarely, if ever, comparable in extent with the differences between any one of them and St. John. Expressed simply, and with the

---

[143] Col. 4.14; II Tim. 4.11; Philem. 24.
[145] Luke 19.43,44; 21.20-24; 23.27-32.
[147] Luke 21.24.

[144] See below, p. 118ff.
[146] Luke 21.20.
[148] Luke 21.23.

reservation that it is always unsafe to generalize, the position is that St. Matthew, St. Mark, and St. Luke, group themselves together on the one side : St. John stands apart on the other.

Some illustration will make this plain. In the first three Gospels the scene of the Ministry is mainly Galilee and the north : in St. John it is Jerusalem and the south—when in St. John Jesus speaks of 'his own country' he means Judaea,[149] whereas in St. Matthew, St. Mark, and St. Luke, He means His own home-town and its neighbourhood.[150] The order of events often differs widely—e.g. the cleansing of the Temple is placed in the first three Gospels at the end of the Ministry,[151] but in St. John almost at the beginning.[152] There are several notable omissions in St. John—there is, for example, no mention of the baptism of Jesus or of the institution of the Eucharist. There are many seemingly unaccountable discrepancies in detail—thus, in St. John, St. Peter is 'from Bethsaida'[153] and not from Capernaum.[154] In the first three Gospels the Words of Jesus are for the most part recorded as pithy sayings and parables, in St. John they nearly always take the form of lengthy discourses[155] and allegories.[156] And finally, the presentation of Jesus and His attitude to certain fundamental questions frequently differs radically—in St. Matthew, St. Mark, and St. Luke, He refuses point-blank to use 'signs' to compel belief,[157] but in St. John His signs are deliberately recorded for their evidential value,[158] and in at least one instance this point of view has the sanction of Jesus Himself.[159]

It would, of course, be a mistake to stress these differences to the neglect of what all four Gospels share in common. All four tell the same story in general outline, because all four are designed to communicate the same 'Gospel' message. Moreover, it will sometimes be found that one or other of the first three agrees on a particular point with St. John against the remaining two (this most frequently happens in the case of St. Luke).[160] The distinction,

---

[149] John. 4.44.   [150] Matt. 13.57; Mark 6.4; Luke 4.24.
[151] Matt. 21.12,13; Mark 11.15-17; Luke 19.45,46.
[152] John 2.13-22.   [153] John 1.44.
[154] Matt. 8.5,14; Mark 1.21,29; Luke 4.31,38.
[155] e.g. John 5.19-47.   [156] e.g. John 10.1-18.
[157] Matt. 12.38,39; Mark 8.11,12; Luke 11.29.
[158] e.g. John 2.11,23; 20.30,31.   [159] John 6.26.
[160] Thus, in St. Luke, the Galilean Ministry ends as early as 9.51, after which the interest is concentrated on Jerusalem, although the scene is not set there : or again, only at Luke 22.50 and John 18.10 is the ear of the High Priest's servant that was cut off said to have been the 'right' ear.

therefore, is not absolute. Nevertheless, there is a distinction.
And it demands an adequate explanation.

Some scholars would emphasize the importance of oral tradition
in this connection. We know, they say, that there was a con-
tinuous 'Gospel' tradition circulating in the early Church by word
of mouth; and they think that the facts are readily explicable if
we suppose that the author of St. John was dependent for his
material upon a different tradition from that on which his predecessors were dependent.

As long ago as the end of the second century St. Clement of
Alexandria wrote as follows:

> 'John, observing that the things obvious to the senses had
> already been set forth in the earlier Gospels, and divinely moved
> by the Holy Spirit, wrote a spiritual Gospel.'[161]

And this explanation is no doubt in essence correct. A study of the
evidence points to the author of St. John having known St. Mark
almost certainly, and St. Luke very probably, though not, it seems,
St. Matthew. Yet such a study also shows that he never used them
in anything like the same way that the authors of St. Matthew and
St. Luke used St. Mark. In short, we are led to the conclusion
that whatever the immediate source of his material, whether he
was drawing on St. Mark or St. Luke, on oral tradition or on his
own personal reminiscences, he throughout selected, re-ordered, and
adapted, that material far more radically than his predecessors, to
serve the theological (what St. Clement calls the 'spiritual') purpose
that inspired his book.

What that purpose was he states at the end. 'Many other signs
therefore,' he writes, 'did Jesus in the presence of his disciples,
which are not written in this book: but these are written, that ye
may believe that Jesus is the Christ, the Son of God; and that
believing ye may have life in his name.'[162]

The truth about Jesus is accordingly proclaimed from the outset.
The Baptist bears witness to His divine mission and declares openly
that He is 'the Son of God'.[163] St. Andrew acknowledges Him
immediately with the words, 'We have found the Messiah'.[164]
St. Philip affirms that He is the fulfilment of the Law and the

---

[161] Quoted by Eusebius, *Hist. Eccl.*, 6.14,7.

[162] John 20.30,31.

[163] John 1.29,34.

[164] John 1.41.

Prophets.[165] Nathaniel confesses, 'Thou art the Son of God; thou art the King of Israel', and Jesus Himself replies, 'Ye shall see the heaven opened, and the angels of God ascending and descending upon the Son of man'.[166] Thus, in the opening chapter all the recognized Messianic titles are gathered together, and no reader can be in any doubt about who Jesus really is, either from His own words, or from the testimony that is borne to Him by others.

And the subsequent chapters sustain this theme. The Ministry is a manifestation of the 'glory' of Jesus, discernible through the 'signs' which He works, and which cause those who are 'of the light' to 'believe' and accept His claim.[167] The claim is advanced in a variety of ways, but especially through the record of the Words of Jesus—'I am the way, the truth, and the life: no one cometh unto the Father but by me'[168] is only one out of many sayings that state the claim directly. And here it is to be observed that divine 'sonship' as applied to Jesus is no empty title given as a matter of form to one who was acknowledged as Messiah: rather does it imply a unity of essence, will, and activity, with the Father-God Himself.[169] In this way the evangelist sets Jesus in the widest context possible. St. Mark sees 'the beginning of the Gospel' in the mission of the Baptist: St. Matthew starts with the birth of Jesus: St. Luke with the birth of the Baptist; but St. John, through the assertion that Jesus was the creative 'Word', goes back to the stage before time was—'In the beginning was the Word . . . all things were made by him . . . and the Word became flesh, and dwelt among us, and we beheld his glory.'[170]

The reason for this manifestation was God's love for man and His concern for man's salvation.[171] Jesus, as 'the only-begotten Son' has revealed to us the Father-God as no other could.[172] As the sacrificial 'lamb' He 'takes away' our sins.[173] As Himself 'the light'[174] He enables those who believe to become 'sons of light'.[175] As 'the resurrection and the life' He is the permanent source of 'eternal life'.[176] And His mission is universal. Through His 'lifting up' on the cross He wills to 'draw all men' unto Him.[177] The Cross, indeed, is His destined 'hour'.[178] He looked forward

[165] John 1.45. [166] John 1.49-51. [167] e.g. John 2.11; 12.35-43.
[168] John 14.6. [169] John 8.16-19; 10.30; 14.8-11. [170] John 1.1,3,14.
[171] John 3.16. [172] John 1.18. [173] John 1.29.
[174] John 8.12. [175] John 12.36. [176] John 11.25,26.
[177] John 12.32. [178] John 17.1.

to it from the first;[179] and at the last He can cry ' It is finished '[180]
—in the sense that the task which the Father has given Him to do
is now accomplished.

On this interpretation of His mission the Resurrection sets, as it
were, an authenticating seal. Henceforward the place of the earthly
Jesus is taken by ' the Comforter, even the Holy Spirit ', whose
function it is to instruct believers, and as ' the Spirit of truth ' to
' guide ' them ' into all truth '.[181] They may, it is true, still retain
the expectation of a final judgement on ' the last day ';[182] but
their fate then is in reality settled now by the fact that they have
already confessed belief in Jesus and have accordingly already
' passed out of death into life '.[183] ' Eternal life ', therefore, is not
to be regarded as a sort of prize to be awarded to the worthy on the
Day of Judgement; it is a state to be enjoyed here and now by
all who so desire. And the condition of enjoyment is belief in Jesus
and His Person—that same belief, of course, which the evangelist
himself tells us he was writing to promote.

By tradition the Gospel is ascribed to St. John, the son of
Zebedee and brother of St. James. It is also said to have been
written at Ephesus, about the end of the first century, when the
writer was a very old man.

And the tradition has much to commend it. The internal evidence of the Gospel is certainly in favour of a late date; while
the peculiar character and manner of presentation of much of the
material contained in it fits in well with the idea that it was the
work of an old man, who had meditated for many years on
the meaning of the events he is describing. If it be pointed out that
this does not prove that he was St. John, the son of Zebedee, the
argument in favour may be stated cumulatively: (1) Since the
Gospel breathes an unmistakably Jewish atmosphere, revealing
especial knowledge of Jewish life and customs,[184] the evangelist
must have been a Jew; (2) His geographical knowledge[185] shows
that he was a Jew of Palestine; (3) His insertion of odd details[186]
must mean that he was frequently an eye-witness of the scenes
described; (4) His references to himself as ' the disciple whom Jesus
loved '[187] admits of no other possibility than that he was St. John,

[179] John 2.4.
[181] John 14.16,17,26; 15.26,27; 16.7-15.
[183] John 5.24.
[185] e.g. John 3.23; 11.18.
[187] e.g. John 13.23; 19.26.

[180] John 19.30.
[182] e.g. John 6.40; 12.48.
[184] e.g. John 4.9; 19.40.
[186] e.g. John 4.6; 19.39.

since of the three disciples whom we know from the other Gospels
to have been most intimate with their Master (St. Peter, St. James,
and St. John),[188] only St. John could have been still living at the
time the Gospel was written. Such a conclusion, furthermore, is
supported by the close association in the later chapters of St. Peter
with 'the disciple whom Jesus loved',[189] an association correspond-
ing with the association between 'Peter and John' in the early
chapters of Acts.[190] It is supported also by the fact that the
evangelist never gives the Baptist his title, but calls him always
simply 'John'.

There are, however, a number of objections to this conclusion.
During the second century the authority of the Gospel was disputed
in some quarters; and this is hardly likely if it had been generally
acknowledged to be the work of the son of Zebedee. Again, when
writing to the Ephesians about the year 115, St. Ignatius has much
to say about St. Paul and his connection with Ephesus, but says
nothing whatever about St. John; which is odd if the tradition
be sound that St. John lived there for many years as 'the great
light' of the local church, and wrote his Gospel there only a few
years previously. Moreover, it is difficult to reconcile the many
outstanding differences between this Gospel and the others if we
suppose that all four are ultimately dependent upon the same source
of information, namely the recollections of the Twelve. And finally,
is it reasonable to suppose that an 'unlearned and ignorant'[191]
Galilean fisherman could have been responsible for such a profound
piece of writing as the Gospel unquestionably is?

No one of these objections, naturally, is decisive in itself. But
taken together they are sufficient to make us pause to ask what
alternatives to the traditional view are possible. And here a variety
of names has been suggested, varying from another of the Lord's
disciples (e.g. St. Philip) at one end to the second-century heretic
Marcion at the other.

The most attractive of these alternatives is the suggestion that
the author was another John. We know from Papias that there
was another John living in Asia at the end of the first century,
whom he distinguished as 'John the Elder'; and Eusebius tells us
that the tomb of this John was an object of reverence at Ephesus
even in his own day.[192] And the suggestion is reinforced by the

---

[188] e.g. Mark 5.37; 9.2. [189] e.g. John 13.24; 20.2. [190] e.g. Acts 3.1; 8.14.
[191] Acts 4.13. [192] Eusebius, *Hist. Eccl.*, 3.39,5 and 6.

consideration that the author of the Gospel was apparently also the author of three Johannine Epistles,[193] and that in the opening verse of the Second and Third Epistles he unambiguously calls himself ' the Elder '.

Some would go further and reconstruct his background and antecedents. He was, they say, undoubtedly an eye-witness, but an eye-witness of only part of the Ministry; for he came from Jerusalem and belonged to one of the aristocratic priestly families there. At the time he was little more than a boy. That is why Jesus, on his visits to Jerusalem, singled him out for special attention, and why his position as ' the disciple whom Jesus loved ' neither excited animosity among the Twelve nor survived in popular memory. But in the life of the young man himself this intimacy with Jesus remained the dominating factor; and, having afterwards moved to Ephesus, he wrote at last his own account, drawing mainly on his own reminiscences and interpreting them in the light of many years spent in pondering their inner meaning. So most, it is said, if not all, of the peculiar features of the Gospel can be accounted for—its manifest Jewish background; the local knowledge of the author, especially of Jerusalem; and, above all, the many differences from the other Gospels, particularly as regards the scene of the Ministry and the author's distinctive outlook.

Such a theory has, of course, the merit of preserving the traditional Ephesian origin of the Gospel, and also the traditional date. It preserves also the traditional author's name. And if we accept it, we have only to suppose that the traditional particularization of the author as ' John, the son of Zebedee ' arose through an easily understandable confusion between the two Johns, both of whom are assured historical figures. We have, therefore, to take the theory seriously. And most would say that it is not merely the most attractive alternative, but also the only satisfactory alternative, to the traditional point of view.

[193] See below, p. 137.

Chapter Five

ACTS, THE GENERAL EPISTLES, AND REVELATION

Acts

ACTS belongs to a class of literature which enjoyed considerable popularity in the early Church, but it is the only example that was received into the New Testament.

Briefly, the book tells the story of the progress of the Gospel, and of the expansion of the Church, from the earliest days in Jerusalem until some thirty years later they were securely established in Rome. 'Ye shall be my witnesses,' the Lord is represented as saying to the disciples at the Ascension, 'both in Jerusalem, and in all Judaea and Samaria, and unto the uttermost part of the earth.'[1] And these words, recorded as they are in the first few verses, may be taken as the programme for the book as a whole.

To begin with, the 'witnesses' are the Twelve. By the descent of the Spirit on the Day of Pentecost they are 'endued with power from on high' for the tasks which lie in front of them; and the narrative, as far as the end of chapter 5, is concerned with their doings in Jerusalem. In chapter 6 seven assistants are appointed, ostensibly to 'serve tables'; but one of them, St. Stephen, proves such an able preacher, and stirs up so much antagonism, that he is condemned by the Jewish authorities and put to death. This is the signal for the first anti-Christian outburst; and in the ensuing persecution believers are 'scattered abroad throughout the regions of Judaea and Samaria'.[2]

The opportunity thus afforded is eagerly seized for preaching;[3] and Philip, another of the seven, has conspicuous success, not only in the city of Samaria itself and the surrounding Samaritan villages,[4] but also in the cities of the Philistine plain 'till he came to Caesarea'.[5] Then Saul, a leader of the persecution, is suddenly

[1] Acts 1.8.   [2] Acts 8.1.   [3] Acts 8.4.   [4] Acts 8.5-25.   [5] Acts 8.26-40.

converted outside the gates of Damascus, and immediately in the Damascus synagogues 'proclaims Jesus' as 'Son of God'.[6]   A preaching tour of St. Peter in the coast land round Caesarea is next recorded : this was noteworthy for the admission to the Church of its first purely Gentile member, the centurion Cornelius.   Meanwhile, the Gospel is spreading northwards, and to lands across the sea; for 'they that were scattered abroad upon the tribulations that arose about Stephen travelled as far as Phoenicia, and Cyprus, and Antioch, speaking the word'.[7]

Henceforward Antioch supplants Jerusalem as the primary centre of interest, and from it all subsequently recorded missionary activity proceeds.   At Antioch 'the disciples were first called Christians'.[8] At Antioch preaching to Gentiles was first undertaken of set purpose.[9]   And it was from Antioch, with the solemn commission of the assembled congregation, that St. Barnabas set out with Saul on the historic journey to Cyprus and Asia Minor.[10]

From chapter 13 onwards the reader's attention is firmly fixed on Saul.   At 13.9 his name is changed to Paul.   By now he has already become a leader—the outstanding leader, in fact, of the whole worldwide Christian mission.   And we follow him on his travels, back to Antioch, again through Asia Minor and on to the mainland of Europe, back again to Antioch, once more through Asia Minor and the European mainland, on his last journey to Jerusalem, and then finally to Rome.   The Church has now expanded, and the Gospel has been carried, from the religious capital of Jewry to the capital of the civilized world.

The plan of Acts is thus straightforward enough.   Like St. Luke it is addressed to Theophilus;[11] and in the opening words the author refers to 'the former treatise I made . . . concerning all that Jesus began both to do and to teach, until the day in which he was received up'.   The reference here is manifestly to the Gospel.   We are to conclude, therefore, that Acts is a continuation of the Gospel, and the work of the same author—St. Luke.

This was the conclusion universally drawn in antiquity; and it is supported by a detailed examination of the books themselves. There are, for instance, a number of words that either are very rare or even do not occur at all elsewhere in the New Testament, but are fairly frequent in St. Luke and Acts—e.g. the verb translated

[6] Acts 9.20.   [7] Acts 11.19.   [8] Acts 11.26.
[9] Acts 11.20.   [10] Acts 13.1-3.   [11] Acts 1.1.

'looking steadfastly' at Acts 1.10 occurs twice in St. Luke, ten times in Acts, but elsewhere in the New Testament only twice (both times in II Cor. 3). Again, characteristic phrases that are found in the Gospel are found again in Acts—thus, the phrase 'as his custom was' is found only at Luke 4.16 and Acts 17.2, and in each case it is connected with entry into a synagogue on the Sabbath. The same author's interests, too, that we observed in 'the former treatise' are discernible also in the latter—the emphasis in Acts on the Gentile Mission, for example, is too obvious to need comment. Altogether, then, we may agree unreservedly that Acts is a continuation of the Gospel, that it was presumably designed as such, and that it was written by St. Luke.

In his Gospel St. Luke used at least two written sources. So we naturally ask, Did he also use written sources in Acts? At first consideration there might seem to be a decided balance in favour on the ground that his method is likely to have been the same for both books. On investigation, however, the analogy breaks down. By the time St. Luke wrote, the term 'Gospel' had a very generally recognized content in Christian circles, and there was plenty of written material available—he himself tells us that as a gospel-writer he had 'many' predecessors.[12] But with his second volume the situation was different. There is nothing whatever to suggest that anyone else before him had ever thought of writing 'Acts'. The whole idea, it seems, was new. And this means that through sheer force of circumstances there would be for Acts no written material available, irrespective of whether the author would have made use of it or not.

Study of the actual text suggests an equally negative answer. Many moderns have spent many years in trying to distinguish sources in Acts; but they have reached no general agreement. Consequently, if we are not prepared to leave the question open, we must admit candidly that so far as the evidence goes it is very definitely against St. Luke's having used written sources for Acts. Rather does it point to his having been indebted, partly to the stories in the churches that he visited with St. Paul, partly to the first-hand accounts given him by the many Christians that he came across himself, and partly to his own personal recollections.

In connection with this last source of information (his own personal recollections) attention should be drawn to the so-called 'we-

12 Luke 1.1.

passages'.   At Acts 16.10 the first personal pronoun 'we' appears, and it continues intermittently until the end of the book.   The effect is to create the impression that the author joined St. Paul at Troas on the second journey and went with him to Philippi: [13] that he stayed at Philippi until St. Paul passed through at the end of the third journey, when he joined him once again: [14] that he was received with St. Paul by the church at Jerusalem; [15] and that he later accompanied him to Rome.[16]   And this is no doubt what happened.   The style of the 'we-passages' is identical with the style of the rest of Acts: they must, therefore, have been written by St. Luke; and we cannot account for them, as some have tried to do, by supposing that he was carelessly incorporating fragments from someone else's diary.   Unless, then, we are willing to believe that he was consciously trying to make us think that he was present on occasions when he was not (a possibility that is most unlikely in view of the unassuming and artless way in which the 'wes' are introduced), we have to take the passages at their face value, and see in them evidence of the participation of St. Luke himself in the events he is describing.

The dating of Acts involves many complications.   If we are satisfied with a date for the Gospel about 80 or 90[17] it might seem an easy matter to assign Acts to the same period, since Acts was apparently written after the Gospel, and probably fairly soon after. But we are at once brought up against the problem raised by the end of Acts, which is inextricably bound up with the date.

The problem is this.   The second half of Acts gives a fairly detailed account of St. Paul's movements and activities, especially in the later chapters.   In these chapters we are told how he was arrested in Jerusalem, how he was imprisoned for three years at Caesarea, and how at last he successfully 'appealed unto Caesar': then follows the excitement of the voyage to Rome and the arrival there; after which the book ends with a picture of St. Paul living for 'two whole years in his own hired dwelling' and 'preaching the kingdom of God . . . none forbidding him'.   Somehow, it seems, the climax is lacking.   After so much preparation we want to know what happened to St. Paul in the end.   Did he appear before Caesar?   If he did, was he condemned or acquitted?   Or if not, what did happen?   We feel instinctively that St. Luke owes

---

[13] Acts 16.10-18.   [14] Acts 20.5,6.   [15] Acts 21.17.
[16] Acts 27.1-28.16.   [17] See above, p. 114.

us an answer to these questions. And the fact that he does not give one leads only to the further question, Why not?

To this question there are three possible answers: (1) that St. Luke tells us no more than he does because at the time he wrote the end of Acts there was nothing more to tell; (2) that he was deliberately reserving the story of St. Paul's trial and execution for the opening chapters of a third volume, which was either never written, or, if written, subsequently lost; (3) that for either literary or apologetic reasons he thought it a bad thing to end with St. Paul's death, preferring instead to finish with a scene of interrupted preaching, which on the one hand illustrated the tranquillity of church life in Rome before the storm of the Neronian persecution, and on the other sounded for the last time the keynote of the entire book.

The first alternative is the simplest; though if we accept it we shall, of course, have to date Acts just over two years after the arrival in Rome—i.e. in 63. A date as early as this would be unexceptionable if Acts stood alone. But it does not stand alone. It is a second volume, and therefore presumably written after the first (St. Luke), which in turn shows incontrovertible evidence of dependence on St. Mark. This means that a date of 63 for Acts carries with it a date of not later than 62 for St. Luke, and a date of not later than 60 for St. Mark. These dates are by no means impossible; but it should be recognized that they are at variance (especially in the case of St. Mark), not only with the general consensus of modern scholarship, but also with the early ecclesiastical tradition.

We turn accordingly to the second alternative which has much to commend it. If St. Luke could write two volumes he may well have written, or contemplated writing, three. And it is pointed out that he appears to look forward to a third volume in the opening words of Acts. There he refers to his Gospel as 'the former treatise'. But the word translated 'former' in this phrase is more accurately rendered 'first' (as the R.V. margin reminds us). Here, then, it is said, is a hint of what was in his mind. Whether or not he ever put his intention into effect it is impossible to know. If he did, and his third volume has been lost, there is no cause for surprise: a great number of early Christian writings were lost— for example, the 'many' attempts to write Gospels made by his predecessors. If he did not, there was doubtless an adequate reason. In either case we are provided with an explanation of why, if he

were writing Acts as late as 80-90, he was content to leave us with
the picture of St. Paul preaching in Rome ' none forbidding him '.
Such a picture makes an excellent end in itself: it also offers an
excellent parallel to the end of the Gospel; for at the end of the
Gospel the Church is securely rooted in Jerusalem, and at the end
of Acts in Rome.

Considerations of this kind seem to have weighed heavily with
St. Luke—which brings us to the third alternative. The more his
interests, motives, and literary methods have been studied of recent
years, the more obvious has it become that he was concerned far
more to select and order his material to promote the causes he had
at heart than simply to record ' what happened ' for its own sake.
In Acts, as we have seen, his main theme is the Gentile Mission;
and it was, apparently, in order to advance the Christian cause by
explaining the nature, origin, and early history of the new Faith
to interested Gentiles that he undertook to write. From this point
of view the details of St. Paul's death were as irrelevant as were
the details of his birth and life as a Jew. Moreover, after taking
considerable pains to show that all through St. Paul's career as a
Christian he had been consistently vindicated by every properly
constituted civil court before which he had been brought,[18] to conclude with an account of his execution in Rome must have seemed
to St. Luke a stultification of his purpose. His primary concern
was with the progress of ' the Gospel ', not with the biography of
St. Paul. Biography was incidental. And so the end of Acts falls
naturally into place. Granted St. Luke's purpose, there could be
no better end, whether he was writing as early as 63 or as late as
85.

THE GENERAL EPISTLES

The term ' General Epistles ' is applied to those New Testament
epistles which are not directly addressed to any particular community of Christians, or to any particular individual, as are the
Epistles of St. Paul, but envisage a more ' general ' type of reader.
They are seven in number—James, I and II Peter, I, II and III John,
and Jude.

James

' James, a servant of God and of the Lord Jesus Christ, to the twelve

[18] e.g. Acts 18.12-17; 26.30-32.

tribes which are of the Dispersion, greeting.'[19]   These opening
words follow the form of introduction usual in New Testament
epistles, but at the end of chapter 5 we miss the customary closing
salutations—an exactly opposite state of affairs to that observable
in Hebrews, which has closing salutations but no epistolary introduction.   And this lack of salutations, combined with the distinctly
vague address to ' the twelve tribes of the Dispersion ', and the complete absence of any personal references anywhere, emphasizes for
us the essentially ' general ' character of James, which, indeed, reads
far more like a homily than a letter.

The subject-matter is Christian behaviour. Temptation, says the
author, is inevitable; but the faithful must endure.[20]   Religion is
not just a matter of giving assent to certain intellectual propositions,
but must show itself in purity of life and good works;[21] and the
practical application of this assertion is illustrated, first by an attack
on the tendency of the rich to lord it over the poor,[22] and then by
reference to the Old Testament to prove that ' faith apart from works
is dead '.[23]   Those who would be teachers have a special obligation
to demonstrate this wisdom in their lives.[24]   Some would make
terms with the world; but this is impossible without falling into
sin.[25]   The possession and the pursuit of riches are particular
snares.[26]   And so, with specific exhortations to the readers to be
patient, to refrain from swearing, to pray frequently and fervently,
to confess their sins to each other, and to convert any that ' do err
from the truth ', the Epistle ends.[27]

The tone throughout is severely practical with a minimum of
theology. That ' God is one ' is an agreed article of faith: [28] He
is also ' Father ',[29] and the source of all good gifts: [30] Jesus is only
mentioned casually as ' the Lord Jesus Christ ';[31] while ' the coming
of the Lord ' in judgement is to be expected very soon,[32] when those
who endure may hope to be ' approved ' and ' receive the crown of
life '.[33]   In short, the Epistle is best described as a homily on the
good life as the author himself conceived it.

He calls himself simply ' James '. Most early Christian writers
that ventured an opinion on the point identified him with ' James,
the Lord's brother ', who was the leader of the church in Jerusalem

[19] Jas. 1.1.   [20] Jas. 1.2-18.   [21] Jas. 1.19-27.
[22] Jas. 2.1-13.   [23] Jas. 2.14-26.   [24] Jas. 3.1-18.
[25] Jas. 4.1-17.   [26] Jas. 5.1-6.   [27] Jas. 5.7-20.
[28] Jas. 2.19.   [29] Jas. 1.27; 3.9.   [30] Jas. 1.5,17.
[31] Jas. 1.1; 2.1.   [32] Jas. 5.7-9.   [33] Jas. 1.12.

from about the year 45 until he was martyred by the Jews in 62.

And with this identification the subject-matter of the Epistle fits admirably; for an unmistakably Palestinian Jewish-Christian colouring pervades the whole. The climatic conditions pre-supposed are those of Palestine:[34] there is mention of ' your synagogue ':[35] the Law and the proper way to keep it is obviously to the writer a matter of primary importance:[36] the theology is barely Christian; while what seem to be echoes of the Words of Jesus are of Words peculiar to the Jewish-Christian Gospel St. Matthew.[37]   On this showing, then, the Epistle will be a circular document, addressed from Jerusalem to the Jewish-Christians of the Dispersion, some-time between 50 and 60.

Objections to this view are two.   In the first place, there was considerable doubt about accepting the Epistle in the early Church: no one in the churches of the East seems to have known it before the beginning of the third century, and no one in the West quotes it before the middle of the fourth—which is very odd if it was indeed a genuine work of ' the Lord's brother '.   And secondly, it is written in very good Greek, and the Old Testament is quoted in the ' Septuagint ' Greek version—which is again odd if it came from St. James of Jerusalem.

Against the second of these objections we may argue that if the Epistle was written to the Dispersion there should really be nothing to surprise us.   In the synagogues of the Dispersion many had no other language than Greek, and the Old Testament was habitually read in Greek for this reason.   It is only to be expected, therefore, that St. James would write in the language his readers knew and quote the version with which they were familiar.   And if we think he was incapable of writing such good Greek, he may well have employed a secretary who ' touched up ' what he dictated, or he may even have written originally in his native Aramaic, and then a translation may have been made by someone else for general circulation.

The first objection, however, is more serious.   If we attach weight to the unwillingness of the early Church to accept the Epistle, it may seem that we shall have to find some other author and another occasion of writing—e.g. an otherwise unknown James (which was,

[34] Jas. 1.11; 5.7.   [35] Jas. 2.2.   [36] Jas. 2.8-13.
[37] Jas. 5.12 and Matt. 5.33-37; cp. also Jas. 5.1-3 and Matt. 6.19-21.

of course, a very common name), who wrote in the period after
the fall of Jerusalem, perhaps as late as 90-100, when the original
Jewish-Christian nucleus of the Church was being more and more
'dispersed', but the primitive theology and practice which Jewish
Christianity represented was still a living force. But there is no
need to be driven as far as this. The fact that the Epistle is a
Jewish-Christian document, whoever wrote it, may have been in
itself sufficient to discredit it in the eyes of Gentile Christians; while
its essentially practical attitude would inevitably make it seem of
little consequence to those whose main interests were theological.
Accordingly, its neglect by the early Church is by no means an
insuperable barrier to accepting the Lord's brother as the author.

I Peter

I Peter resembles Hebrews in being a 'word of exhortation'
addressed to Christians who are being persecuted. The circumstances, naturally, are different—for one thing the persecution
referred to in I Peter seems to have been much more severe than
that to which 'the Hebrews' were subjected. But in much the
same way the author seeks to provide his readers with a theology
that will help them to stand the strain; while he is at constant pains
to ensure that they shall never through misbehaviour give any
handle to their detractors. Indeed, he argues that the truly Christ-
like life of individual Christians is the best refutation there is of
charges falsely made: it may even have the effect of softening the
hearts of many, and perhaps of converting some, whose anti-
Christian violence is due primarily to ignorance of what Christianity
really is.

After the customary introductory salutations the Epistle opens
with some words of thanksgiving for the Lord's Resurrection, which
is the source of the new life of Christians and of the power which
enables them to endure their 'manifold temptations'.[38] Their calling is to holiness and obedience, rooted in, and exemplified by, the
Passion of the Lord Himself.[39] They should, therefore, behave at
all times in a manner befitting 'the people of God';[40] and specific
injunctions are given to this end[41]—above all that they should suffer
as Christ suffered without complaint or reviling, 'because Christ

[38] I Pet. 1.3-12.   [39] I Pet. 1.13-25.
[40] I Pet. 2.1-10.   [41] I Pet. 2.11-3.12.

I

also suffered for you, leaving you an example, that ye should follow his steps'.[42]

This leads to an exposition of the writer's theology of suffering, in which the sufferings of Christians are linked with the sufferings of Christ, and all are shown to be part of the divine scheme of redemption. Just as Christ was 'put to death in the flesh but quickened in the spirit', so Christians share in the Passion and Resurrection of their Lord. Of this sharing baptism (as in Romans[43]) is at once the outward symbol and the inward guarantee. Christ is now 'on the right hand of God'. Christians are still 'suffering in the flesh'. But 'the end of all things is at hand'. It is consequently the duty of Christians to 'arm' themselves with 'the same mind' that was in Christ: to face 'the fiery trial' as something only to be expected as the prelude to the End; and to 'rejoice' because they are made 'partakers of Christ's sufferings' now, so that later, 'at the revelation of his glory', they may also 'rejoice with exceeding joy'.[44]

Then, those in posts of special responsibility in the ministry, and again all Christians generally, are exhorted to fulfil their obligations in a spirit of humility while awaiting the final consummation.[45] And the Epistle ends with three verses of salutations.[46]

The prevailing view that it was written by St. Peter to persecuted Christians in the north-western provinces of Asia Minor derives, of course, from the address—'Peter, an apostle of Jesus Christ, to the elect who are sojourners of the Dispersion in Pontus, Galatia, Cappadocia, Asia, and Bithynia'.[47] It is also pointed out that the writer calls himself 'a witness of the sufferings of Christ',[48] which St. Peter undoubtedly was: that he associates himself closely with St. Mark,[49] which is supported by the ecclesiastical tradition about the origin of St. Mark's Gospel;[50] and that there are several significant agreements between the Epistle and the sermons of St. Peter recorded in Acts—for example, in both Jesus is identified with the Suffering Servant of Isaiah 53 in terms far more explicit than any found elsewhere in the New Testament.[51] If then, as is usually thought, St. Peter was martyred at Rome in the persecution under Nero which broke out in August 64, we are presented with a set of circumstances that seems to fit the contents of the Epistle very

[42] I Pet. 2.21. [43] Rom. 6.1-11. [44] I Pet. 3.13-4.19.
[45] I Pet. 5.1-11. [46] I Pet. 5.12-14. [47] I Pet. 1.1.
[48] I Pet. 5.1. [49] I Pet. 5.13. [50] See above, p. 102.
[51] I Pet. 2.21-25 and Acts 3.13,26; 4.27,30: cp. also I Pet. 4.5 with Acts 10.42.

well. The Emperor and his henchmen have initiated 'the fiery trial'; and St. Peter from 'Babylon'[52] (a cryptic reference, we must suppose, to Rome) writes a brief word of exhortation[53] to those Christians in Asia Minor, for whom he felt himself responsible, not long before his death.

But, as we have noted with other New Testament writings, the prevailing view is not without its difficulties. Traces of the Epistle in western Christendom are scanty during the first three centuries: the style is very good Greek, far better than we should have expected St. Peter to be able to write; and there are a number of curiously close parallels between this Epistle and others—especially Romans[54] and James.[55] Again, it is surprising that if St. Peter really were writing from Rome at this time he should say nothing about St. Paul, although he was apparently writing from within the same Christian circle:[56] it is equally surprising that if the persecution had already begun he should give no details about it: it is still more surprising that in such a situation he should calmly bid his readers, 'Be subject to every ordinance of men', and, in particular, 'Honour the king' (i.e. Nero himself).[57] Moreover, there is no reason for thinking that Nero's persecution affected any area outside Rome and its immediate neighbourhood: it is questionable whether St. Peter as 'the apostle of the circumcision'[58] would have felt himself responsible for Christians who were at any rate predominantly Gentile;[59] and in any case, would St. Peter, in addressing 'elders', refer to himself simply as a 'fellow-elder'?[60]

Each of these points can be answered satisfactorily. Thus, we may say that in referring to himself as a 'fellow-elder' St. Peter was practising the humility that he preached: that we have no right to question that he worked among Gentiles, since of his later evangelistic activities we know next to nothing; and that the Neronian persecution may well have spread to Asia Minor although there is no evidence that it did, or alternatively, even if it did not, St. Peter in Rome may well have thought that it would. The injunction to 'Honour the king' may readily be explained as due

---

[52] I Pet. 5.13.   [53] I Pet. 5.12.
[54] Cp. I Pet. 2.6-8 with Rom. 9.32,33; I Pet. 2.13-17 with Rom. 13.1-7; I Pet. 3.8,9 with Rom. 12.16,17.
[55] Cp. 'Dispersion' (I Pet. 1.1 and Jas. 1.1); 'manifold temptations' (I Pet. 1.6 and Jas. 1.2); 'the proof of your faith' (I Pet. 1.7 and Jas. 1.3); and I Pet. 5.5,6 with Jas. 4.6-9.
[56] Cp. I Pet. 5.13 with Col. 4.10 and Philem. 24.
[57] I Pet. 2.13-17.   [58] Gal. 2.8.   [59] e.g. I Pet. 2.9,10; 4.2,3.   [60] I Pet. 5.1.

to his anxiety that no pretext should be given for a charge that Christians were revolutionaries: he may have thought that his readers would have heard quite enough about what was going on at Rome; while the fact that he does not mention St. Paul may be countered by the equally significant (or insignificant) fact that in the salutations of Colossians and Philemon St. Paul makes no mention of St. Peter. The parallelisms between the Epistle and other epistles may easily be due to the circulation in the early Church of collections of proof-texts, exhortations to good behaviour, and other material of an instructional character, which different writers would draw upon as required, with the result that there was bound to be much common subject-matter and phraseology: the good Greek may be attributed to Silvanus (i.e. St. Silas), who is named as St. Peter's secretary,[61] and who may have had a far greater share in the composition of the Epistle than the casual reader might suspect; and finally, the scant traces of the Epistle in the West in early times should occasion no surprise, for it is usual for any letter to be better known in the region it is addressed to than in the district from which it comes.

The prevailing view, therefore, is eminently defensible—provided, that is, that we are prepared to regard the Epistle as the joint work of St. Peter and St. Silas, in spite of the latter's name not appearing in the opening salutation as it does in the opening salutations of I and II Thessalonians.

If we are not convinced, a number of possibilities are opened up. Many of those who deny St. Peter's connection with the Epistle altogether approach the problem from the angle of date. It is clear from the Epistle, they say, that the Christians of north-western Asia Minor were being persecuted merely because they were Christians.[62] Attempts are accordingly made to fix the date when the Roman Empire first made the profession of Christianity illegal; for it is this situation, it is maintained, that is presupposed by the terms in which the author writes. Unfortunately, however, no agreement about this date has been reached. In any event, it is extremely doubtful whether the language of the Epistle will bear the weight of the interpretation thus thrust upon it. There is no sure ground for asserting that the persecution referred to was anything but local; and spasmodic, local, persecutions of Christians, as Christians, were common enough from the days of St. Stephen onwards. The situa-

[61] I Pet. 5.12.　　　　　　　　[62] e.g. I Pet. 4.16.

tion described in the Epistle may in consequence be related to any outbreak of anti-Christian violence at any time between the mid-first and mid-second centuries.   And this period, so far as our knowledge of what happened in north-western Asia Minor is concerned, is one of considerable obscurity.

A more profitable approach is from the angle of authorship.   Since the Epistle expressly states that it is the work of St. Peter, we must suppose that, if it is not, someone must have designedly written under St. Peter's name.   But the Epistle betrays nowhere any traces of what might be called ' forgery '.   On the contrary, it is as straightforward and unaffected a piece of writing as is found anywhere in the New Testament.   There is much, therefore, to be said for the suggestion that the author himself did not write under the name of St. Peter, and that the crucial verses which imply that he did (the opening and concluding salutations) are additions by a later editor. On this view, some second-century Christian, desiring to secure the widest possible circulation for what seemed to him something of the utmost value, hit on the device of adding to the original two extra verses at the beginning and three more at the end, and thus succeeded in investing an inherently valuable, and probably anonymous, document with the authority of an apostolic epistle.

Not all scholars who take this view, however, are satisfied that the original document is a unity.   Study of the style leaves no room for doubt that it is all by the same author.   But there is a decided break at 4.11.   Some accordingly think that 1.3-4.11 was delivered as a sermon to a group of newly baptized converts by the elder who had baptized them, and that 4.12-5.11 was a letter written later by the same elder to meet an outbreak of persecution.

To discuss the details of such a position would be out of place here.   It would also be out of place to try and identify the elder. Suffice it to say that Aristion of Smyrna (*circa* 90-95) is the most ingenious guess that has so far been made.   But it should be emphasized that this is no more than a guess.   For the truth is that, if we are not satisfied with St. Peter and St. Silas as joint authors, we can do nothing else but guess.

II Peter and Jude

These two epistles are taken together since there is obviously some sort of literary relationship between them.   We have only to look at the references in the margin of the Revised Version to see that II Pet. 2.1-3.3 and Jude 4-18 are parallel almost verse by verse. Is one, then, dependent on the other? Or have both drawn from a common source? And if one is dependent on the other, which is dependent on which?

That both have drawn from a common source is in theory possible enough. But on investigation it is found that if the common matter is removed from Jude there is very little left, which must mean that the supposed common source was almost identical with the Jude we know to-day. And to admit this is in practice tantamount to preferring one form of the alternative hypothesis—namely, that II Peter was dependent on Jude.

It is in fact this form of the alternative which is generally preferred. II Peter is much longer than Jude; and since the tendency in the early Church was towards expansion rather than the reverse (as we saw in the Gospels), it is more likely that the author of II Peter expanded Jude than that the author of Jude curtailed II Peter. A comparison of styles reinforces this point. The style of Jude is certainly the fresher and the more vigorous of the two—thus, the author starts off without the long introduction that is found in II Peter, and in his reference to The Assumption of Moses he quotes exactly (' great swelling words '[63]) whereas II Peter has an explanatory addition ('great swelling words of vanity ').[64] Moreover, if the author of Jude were dependent on II Peter we should expect him to refer to St. Peter by name instead of rather vaguely bidding his readers ' remember the words which have been spoken by the apostles of our Lord Jesus Christ ': [65] on the other hand, however, the author of II Peter is most concerned to claim not only apostolic, but especially Petrine, sanction for his admonitions.[66] There can be little doubt, therefore, on which side the dependence lies.

Jude is a tract against heresy—a self-confessed exhortation ' to contend earnestly for the faith once for all delivered to the saints ' in opposition to false teachers.[67] The dangers of unbelief and wrong belief are explained by reference to previous judgements;[68] and the readers are warned not to be led astray.[69] There are the normal epistolary introductions and conclusions. Otherwise, the Epistle is only noteworthy for its quotations from The Assumption

---

[63] Jude 16.   [64] II Pet. 2.18.   [65] Jude 17.   [66] e.g. II Pet. 1.15-18; 3.1.
[67] Jude 3,4.   [68] Jude 5-16.   [69] Jude 17-23.

of Moses[70] and Enoch,[71] and also for its rather rudimentary theology—God is 'Father'[72] and 'Saviour':[73] Jesus Christ is 'Lord'[74] and 'Master';[75] and faithful Christians, inspired by the Spirit,[76] may look forward to 'eternal life'[77] in the presence of God's glory.[78]

Both these last points might be cited in favour of regarding the Epistle as the work of 'Judas, a servant of Jesus Christ, and brother of James'.[79] To no Christian anywhere were books like The Assumption of Moses and Enoch likely to be better known than to the Jewish-Christians of Palestine; while the rudimentary theology corresponds exactly with what we have already observed in James. If, then, we may attribute the Epistle to another of the Lord's brothers, we shall suppose that it was written from either Palestine or Syria as a general warning against doctrinal developments of which the author disapproved, some time between 60 and 85.

Some, however, are of the opinion that the words 'brother of James' in the opening salutation are a later addition, and that the writer was an unknown Jude who wrote in the first half of the second century. They argue for this date, partly because they think that the writer seems to look back to the formative 'apostolic' period as if it were long since past,[80] and partly because they think that the type of false teaching attacked was not current as early as the first century. The former of these considerations has something to be said for it; but about the latter we can only say, if we are honest, that the evidence is insufficient either to confirm such an opinion or to disprove it. The writer's acquaintance with the Septuagint, too, has been held to point to a place of origin outside Palestine—perhaps to Alexandria: but here again acquaintance with the Septuagint is far too slight a foundation on which to build any argument of substance. Similarly, the fact that many in the early Church rejected the Epistle is in this case of minor significance, since St. Jerome (†420) expressly says that they did so because it quoted Enoch.

The final decision, therefore, may equally well go either way. But on balance it is probably true to say that the scales incline slightly in favour of 'Jude the brother of James'.

[70] Jude 9,16,18.   [71] Jude 6,14.   [72] Jude 1.   [73] Jude 25.
[74] Jude 4,17,21.   [75] Jude 4.   [76] Jude 19,20.   [77] Jude 21,
[78] Jude 24.   [79] Jude 1.   [80] Jude 3,17,20,

If there is one thing certain about II Peter it is that it was not written by St. Peter. There is no trace whatever of the Epistle until fairly late in the second century. Long after this it was an object of dispute—St. Jerome, about 400, says, 'It is disputed by the majority'.[81] The writer protests far too much that he is St. Peter, not only in the opening address, but also later when he claims that he was present at the Transfiguration,[82] that 'this is now, beloved, the second epistle that I write unto you',[83] and that he regards St. Paul as a 'brother'.[84] Furthermore, his dependence on Jude is decisive.

Who the writer was it is impossible to determine. That he should refer to a collection of St. Paul's letters, 'wherein are some things hard to be understood, which the ignorant and unsteadfast wrest, as they do also the other scriptures',[85] must mean that he was writing well on in the second century when the Pauline Epistles were ranked as 'scripture' and their interpretation occasioned controversy. But no precise date can be fixed. Nor is there any indication of any place of origin.

But it is clear that he was as concerned as was the author of Jude to safeguard what he conceived to be purity of doctrine, since the body of the Epistle merely recapitulates his predecessor's warnings. To the material he derived from Jude he prefixes a comparatively lengthy introduction, urging his readers to make their 'calling and election sure', and reminding them (in his role of St. Peter) that he is a fit and proper person to do so;[86] and afterwards he adds a special section on the final consummation,[87] before ending with some more admonitions.[88]

It is this section on the final consummation that gives II Peter its primary interest. There are those who say, 'Where is the promise of his coming? for, from the day that the fathers fell asleep, all things continue as they were.' St. Paul had previously had to deal with much the same question when writing to the Thessalonians:[89] so had the writer of Hebrews;[90] and so had other New Testament writers.[91] Christians had been taught to look forward to the Day. But the Day had not arrived. And the longer they waited the more pressing did the problem become.

Our writer's answer had already been adumbrated in the Alexan-

---

[81] Jerome, *De viris illustribus*, 1.   [82] II Pet. 1.15-18.   [83] II Pet. 3.1.
[84] II Pet. 3.15.   [85] II Pet. 3.16.   [86] II Pet. 1.1-21.
[87] II Pet. 3.3-13.   [88] II Pet. 3.14-18.   [89] See above, p. 33.
[90] See above, p. 78.   [91] See e.g., p. 113.

drian Jewish book known as Slavonic Enoch,[92] and perhaps also in some Christian writings—e.g. The Epistle of Barnabas.[93] It is that, since, according to Ps. 90.4 'one day is with the Lord as a thousand years, and a thousand years as one day', we must see time as God Himself sees it, and not be impatient. God is not 'slack'. The Day will surely come 'as a thief'. Then the whole Universe will be dissolved in fire. The Judgement will involve the 'destruction of ungodly men'; while the faithful can confidently expect to participate in the joys of 'new heavens and a new earth'. This answer, of course, is fundamentally no more than a second century re-affirmation of the central hope of the primitive Gospel. But the point about the 'thousand years', so far as the New Testament is concerned, is new.

I, II and III John

No fresh problems of authorship are raised by these Epistles. The tradition in the Church is definite; and the evidence provided by the constant recurrence of the same words, phrases, and ideas, is conclusive, not only that all three are the work of the same author,[94] but also that that author was the author of St. John.[95] Whatever view, therefore, we take about the authorship of the Gospel will apply equally to the Epistles. The only need now is to give some account of the probable circumstances of their origin.

In this respect the First Epistle is not very helpful on account of its exceedingly 'general' character. There is no indication who the readers were: they are described merely as the author's 'little children' and 'beloved'. But the main purpose in writing was clearly to drive home the message of the Gospel[96] by inculcating, on the one hand true belief,[97] and on the other truly Christian behaviour as the fruit of true belief.[98] The particular error that seems to have threatened the readers was the denial that 'Jesus is the Christ'[99] and that he had 'come in the flesh'[100]—in other words, the repudiation of the whole doctrine of Incarnation (i.e. 'becoming flesh'). We know that in the second century there were many all over the Christian world who thought the flesh much

[92] Slav. Enoch, 32 and 33.   [93] Barn. 15.
[94] Cp. e.g. I John 2.7 with II John 5; II John 4 with III John 3,4.
[95] Cp. e.g. I John 3.11 with John 13.34; II John 12 with John 15.11; III John 12 with John 21.24.
[96] I John 1.1-4.   [97] e.g. I John 4.1-6.   [98] e.g. I John 4.7-21.
[99] I John 2.22.   [100] I John 4.2.

too frail and sinful a medium for the manifestation of the Son of God, and who taught in consequence that Jesus had not really taken flesh but merely 'seemed' to do so. If, then, we are right in dating all three Johannine Epistles within the first century (which is inevitable if they are by the same author as the Gospel), we may see in the 'liars' and 'false prophets' attacked references to the earliest known disseminators of the well-known Docetic (i.e. 'seeming') heresy. And since both the Gospel and its author are associated with Ephesus, it is natural to associate the Epistles with Ephesus too. Whether the First Epistle was written before or after the Gospel we cannot say. It has been suggested, with some plausibility, that it dates from about the same time, and that it was written as a sort of covering letter, designed partly to commend the Gospel as an interpretation of the inner meaning of the Lord's earthly life, and partly also to draw out the practical implications of the teaching contained in it.

In its central section the Second Epistle exhibits exactly the same concern for purity of doctrine and innocency of life.[101] But it is much shorter than the First Epistle. Moreover, it obviously has a more limited objective. It is written by 'the elder unto the elect lady and her children':[102] the writer has 'many things' to communicate, but he prefers to leave them for the present until he has opportunity for a visit;[103] and he sends greetings from 'the children of thine elect sister'.[104] We may, if we will, understand 'the elect lady', 'thine elect sister', and their 'children', as referring to two unnamed sisters with their families. More probably, however, the references are to two churches and their members. In that case 'the children of thine elect sister' are likely to be the Christians of Ephesus, and 'the elect lady and her children' the members of the church to which the Epistle was addressed—one of the churches, no doubt, in the neighbourhood of Ephesus, such as Smyrna or Sardis, over which the Elder exercised a general oversight.

The Third Epistle is more specific still. Like Philemon it is a letter to an individual—'the elder unto Gaius'.[105] The subject is the reception in Gaius's own church of certain 'brethren and strangers', who are apparently missionaries and working with the approval, if not under the direct authority, of the writer.[106] He says that he has already written on the matter 'unto the church',

---

[101] II John 4-11.   [102] II John 1.   [103] II John 12.
[104] II John 13.   [105] III John 1.   [106] III John 5-8.

but the self-assertive Diotrephes (an official, it seems, of this church) is antagonistic to him on personal grounds and has carried his antagonism to the extent of refusing to 'receive the brethren': but he hopes to come soon himself and set Diotrephes firmly in his place.[107] Meanwhile, Gaius is to 'imitate . . . that which is good' and await his arrival.[108] Whether or not the church to which Gaius and Diotrephes belonged was the same church as that to which the Second Epistle was addressed is debatable. Probably it was not. But in any event the Third Epistle makes it plain that the Elder's standing was recognized in at least one church other than his own, even though an isolated individual might presume to question it.

Revelation

Revelation shares with Acts the distinction of being the sole representative of its literary class in the New Testament. But whereas St. Luke in writing Acts was an innovator, the author of Revelation was not. When he wrote there were a number of Jewish 'revelations' (usually called 'apocalypses') already in existence, the best known being Daniel in the Old Testament, II Esdras in the Apocrypha, and Enoch, which, as we have observed, is quoted in Jude.

The basic idea of this class of literature is that the course of history is predetermined by God. Ordinary human beings can do no more than guess what the future holds. But every now and then God reveals to a chosen prophet or 'seer' through visions (the meaning of which is normally explained by an attendant angel) 'the things which must shortly come to pass'. The interest is for the most part concentrated on the final consummation, for this is not only the end of history, but also the ultimate unveiling and vindication of the plan and the justice of God. To the early Christians, therefore, whose faith and hope were centred on the future and the coming of the Day, as was the faith and hope of so many of their Jewish neighbours, this type of literature was bound to make a strong appeal. And the wonder is not that one, but that only one, 'apocalyptic' writing is to be found in the New Testament.

In form the book follows closely the accepted Jewish model. The author's name is given in the opening verses, followed immediately by an account of the circumstances of the revelation.[109] Then

---

[107] III John 9,10.   [108] III John 11-14.   [109] Rev. 1.1-20.

comes a group of warning 'letters' to the seven churches of Asia Minor, starting with Ephesus.[110]   A series of visions occupies the body of the book.[111]   And the whole is rounded off with an epilogue, emphasizing both the immediacy of the End and the need for readiness on the part of the readers to meet it.[112]

The situation and the message are easily summarized.   The churches of Asia Minor, while awaiting the End, are experiencing persecution for 'the word of God and the testimony of Jesus'.[113] The persecution has been brought on because Christians refuse to take part in the widespread worship of the Roman Emperor, which for them is apostasy.[114]   The writer enjoins his readers to stand firm.[115]   Their sufferings are all part of the divinely appointed signs of the End.[116]   Soon the Lord will come.[117]   The Judgement will take place.[118]   The wicked will be consigned to 'the lake of fire'.[119] And the righteous will dwell with God in the 'new heaven' and the 'new earth', where free from all pain and fear of death they will 'reign for ever and ever'.[120]

Revelation is thus intimately concerned with a persecution in Asia Minor.   The scene of the author's visions is stated to be the island of Patmos,[121] just off the coast of Asia Minor, about fifteen miles from Ephesus, where he was imprisoned during the persecution. And his name is given as John.[122]

In the early Church it was customary to identify this John with the son of Zebedee, author of the Gospel and the three Johannine Epistles.   But the identification was by no means universal.   Some, indeed, repudiated Revelation altogether and said it was written by the heretic Cerinthus under an assumed name—mainly, it seems, because they did not like what was in it.   The objections, however, of such a man as Dionysius, who was bishop of Alexandria in the middle of the third century and who is quoted at length by Eusebius with obvious approval,[123] are in a different category.   They are, in fact, exactly the kind of objections that weigh with us to-day.

Dionysius takes his stand firmly on the grounds of style and language.   The Gospel and Epistles, he points out, have obviously much in common: no author's name is mentioned in any of them:

[110] Rev. 2.1-3.22.   [111] Rev. 4.1-22.5.   [112] Rev. 22.6-21.
[113] e.g. Rev. 1.9; 6.9.   [114] Rev. 2.13; 14.9; 20.4.   [115] e.g. Rev. 3.11; 22.12.
[116] e.g. Rev. 16.1-21.   [117] e.g. Rev. 1.7; 22.20.   [118] Rev. 20.4-13.
[119] Rev. 20.15.   [120] Rev. 21.1-22.5.   [121] Rev. 1.9.
[122] Rev. 1.1,4,9; 22.8.   [123] Eusebius, *Hist. Eccl.*, 7.25.

the beginning of the First Epistle very closely resembles the beginning of the Gospel; and the same words and phrases (such as 'life', 'light', and 'the commandment' that we should 'love one another') are to be found throughout. Revelation, on the other hand, is utterly different: the author's name is mentioned both at the beginning and the end: in the body of the book there is 'scarcely a syllable in common' with either the Gospel or the Epistles; and whereas both Gospel and Epistles are 'written in faultless Greek and exhibit the greatest literary skill', the 'style' of the author of Revelation and 'his use of the Greek language is not accurate, for he employs barbarous idioms and in some places commits downright solecisms'. From this Dionysius infers diversity of authorship. He observes further that the author of Revelation calls himself simply 'John' and neither makes any claim nor gives any hint that he was the son of Zebedee. And since John was a very common name among Christians, and since there were in his own day two tombs at Ephesus 'each said to be John's', he finds no difficulty in attributing Revelation to a second John.

To the modern student the linguistic argument used by Dionysius is decisive—it is inconceivable, for example, that the same writer, when referring to Jesus as 'the Lamb', should have used the Greek word *amnos* in the Gospel[124] but *arnion* in Revelation.[125] But undoubtedly Dionysius went too far in saying that the two books 'have scarcely a syllable in common'. In spite of the many, and incontrovertible, linguistic differences, there are also certain agreements, particularly in underlying theological ideas, which must be taken into account as well. Thus, St. John and Revelation are the only two books in the New Testament to call Jesus 'the Word of God';[126] or, again, they are the only two which explicitly apply to him the title 'the Lamb'. We are justified, therefore, in concluding that although they cannot have been written by the same author they are nevertheless products of the same school.

Any further attempt to identify our author will depend, of course, on what we think about the authorship of the Gospel and the three Epistles. If we are satisfied with the traditional view that they are the work of the son of Zebedee, we shall, like Dionysius, attribute Revelation to another John—in all probability to 'John the Elder', whom we know to have been a 'great light' in the Christian com-

[124] John 1.29,36.   [125] e.g. Rev. 5.6,8,12,13.   [126] John 1.1,14; Rev. 19.13.

munity at Ephesus in the latter part of the first century. If, on the other hand, we prefer the theory that he, and not the son of Zebedee, was the author of the Gospel and Epistles, then we shall attribute Revelation either to the son of Zebedee, or to a third John, whom we may distinguish as 'John the Seer'.

At first sight the attribution to the son of Zebedee has much to commend it, since the essentially Jewish background and form of the book, together with much of its contents and the general 'barbarism' of its contents, seem to suit very well an author who had been bred and brought up in the Judaism of Palestine. But we still have to reckon with Dionysius's point that there is no claim, or even hint, in the book itself that the author was the son of Zebedee. Not only are there no references to the Lord's earthly life that sound as if they came from an eye-witness; but the writer refers to himself simply as one of the 'servants' of God and of the company of Christian 'prophets',[127] and when he mentions 'the twelve apostles of the Lamb'[128] he does so in a manner which implies that he himself was not of their number. In the circumstances, therefore, it is best to go no further than the evidence warrants, and to be content with 'John the Seer'.

Of the date and details of the persecution in which he suffered we have no sure knowledge beyond what can be derived from his own allusions. The persecution was certainly severe, for many Christians had been martyred;[129] and it was equally certainly connected with their refusal to worship the Emperor.[130] But whether it was confined to Asia Minor or not does not appear. Some would assign it to the reign of Nero and regard it as an extension to the provinces of the persecution which broke out after the fire at Rome in 64: others would number it among the many acts of savagery perpetrated in his concluding years by Domitian (81-96); and yet others would relate it to the persecution in Bithynia, in northern Asia Minor, about which the governor Pliny corresponded with the Emperor Trajan in 112. The external evidence unfortunately does not materially help us. As we saw when dealing with I Peter, there is no reason for thinking that the persecution under Nero spread outside Rome and its immediate neighbourhood. Nor, again, is there any reason for thinking, either that Domitian ever persecuted Christians as such, or that the persecution in Bithynia which

---

[127] Rev. 22.9.
[129] e.g. Rev. 6.9; 12.11; 18.24.

[128] Rev. 21.14.
[130] Rev. 2.13; 14.9; 20.4.

Pliny describes was anything like so severe as the persecution reflected in Revelation.

On the whole, however, the Domitianic date has most in its favour. It was Domitian who first enforced Emperor-worship rigorously throughout the Roman Empire. And it was, moreover, to the last years of his reign that Revelation was almost unanimously assigned in the Church.

Chapter Six

THE IDEA OF A NEW TESTAMENT
AND THE GROWTH
OF THE NEW TESTAMENT CANON

THE BOOKS of the New Testament were originally separate
entities and in Chapters II-V they have been treated separately. In
this concluding chapter, however, we shall try to see how they
became associated together, at first as components of an increasingly more generally accepted collection of early Christian writings,
and then finally as an authoritative 'New' Testament, which the
Church by universal consent added to what she now called the
'Old' Testament inherited from Judaism.

As previously, we may begin with St. Paul's Epistles.

St. Paul wrote, as we have seen, to particular churches and particular individuals, about particular problems, on particular occasions. It was only natural that many of the churches and individuals
to whom he wrote should keep his letters and treasure them. Not
that there is any reason for thinking that all his letters were kept,
or that they were all treasured equally if they were kept. On the
contrary, it is probable that in the ordinary course of events a
number were lost; while some, perhaps, were deliberately suppressed
because the recipients did not like what was in them. But St. Paul
was one of the great leaders of the early Church; and he ended his
life as a martyr. As the years went by, therefore, and his work
and achievement were more clearly seen in their true proportions,
anything that he had written was bound to be accorded even greater
respect and reverence merely because he had written it. And whatever may have been the first reaction of a church or an individual
to a letter from St. Paul, the time soon came when to have received
one at all was in itself a claim to distinction. Consequently, from
the last decade of the first century onwards there were the strongest

possible motives at work for the preservation of St. Paul's correspondence. To the letter, or letters, written to themselves many churches added copies of letters written to others, and at the same time despatched copies of their own letters elsewhere whenever they were asked for. Thus collections of St. Paul's letters were formed; and church came to vie with church for the possession of the most complete collection obtainable.

For the origin of this system of exchange between churches St. Paul himself seems to have been at least partly responsible. 'And when this epistle hath been read among you,' he writes to the Colossians, 'cause that it be read also in the church of the Laodiceans; and that ye also read the epistle from Laodicea.'[1] However we may choose to interpret 'the Epistle from Laodicea' here,[2] it is certain that St. Paul was thinking in terms of an exchange between Colossae and Laodicea. And the procedure which he explicitly recommends in this instance was subsequently widely adopted. About the year 110 St. Ignatius, bishop of Antioch, on his way through Asia Minor to his own martyrdom at Rome, himself wrote a letter to the church of Ephesus, and in it he refers the Ephesians to the example of 'Paul . . . who in every epistle makes mention of you in Christ Jesus':[3] so St. Ignatius, obviously, was familiar with at any rate several letters of St. Paul. Similarly, the author of II Peter, writing later,[4] reminds his readers of 'our beloved brother Paul', who 'wrote unto you . . . in all his epistles . . . things hard to be understood':[5] once again there is evidence of the existence of a Pauline collection familiar to both writer and readers.

The earliest Pauline collection that we know anything definite about is the collection made by the heretic Marcion in the middle of the second century. Marcion was the son of the bishop of Sinope in Pontus, the most northerly province in Asia Minor; and he migrated to Rome about 140. After a few years there he began to disseminate unorthodox teaching. Puzzled by the many apparent contradictions between 'the Law' and the 'Gospel' (such, for example, as the obvious contrast between 'An eye for an eye and a tooth for a tooth'[6] and 'To him that smiteth thee on the one cheek offer also the other'[7]), Marcion came eventually to the conclusion

[1] Col. 4.16. [2] See above, pp. 63, 64, 70. [3] Ignatius, *Eph.*, 12.2.
[4] On the date of II Peter see above, p. 136.
[5] II Pet. 3.15,16. [6] Ex. 21.24. [7] Luke 6.29.

K

that they were of different origin and derived from two different gods. The Law, he affirmed, was the work of an inferior god, the god of the Jews, whose interest was only in justice—'The Just God': the Gospel, on the other hand, was the revelation of the Supreme God, the God of Christians—'the Good God', whose nature was love. There was, therefore, no kind of relationship between Christianity and Judaism whatever. The two were completely opposed. Anyone who maintained the opposite was perverting the genuine Gospel. And in his book *Antitheses* Marcion worked out this position in detail.

Such a startling repudiation of what the Church had always taught was, of course, immediately condemned, and Marcion and his followers were excommunicated. What concerns us now, however, is not Marcion's personal history but his interest in St. Paul. According to Marcion, Jesus of Nazareth was sent by 'the Good God' to deliver men from the bondage of 'the Just God', who had enslaved them by the ordinances of the Law: the Gospel of Jesus was 'new wine' which could not be forced without disaster into the 'old wineskins' of Judaism. And none of the disciples had realized this, so Marcion maintained, except St. Paul. St. Paul was, therefore, to him the only truly Christian apostle, and his epistles the only reliable guide from which to find out what Christianity really was.

Consequently, in his *Apostolicum* (i.e. his collection of St. Paul's Epistles) Marcion put Galatians first; for this is unquestionably the most anti-Jewish of all the Pauline letters, containing such passages as 'For freedom did Christ set us free: stand fast therefore, and be not entangled again in a yoke of bondage',[8] which seemed to Marcion to conform with his own ideas exactly. Next in order to Galatians came I and II Corinthians: then Romans: then I and II Thessalonians: then 'Laodiceans' (=Ephesians);[9] and then finally Colossians, Philippians, and Philemon. From this list it will be seen that Marcion's collection contained only ten of the now extant epistles. Whether he knew of others, and rejected them, is uncertain. What is certain, however, is that he took considerable liberties with the text, excising or altering what he found uncongenial— thus, the four verses Gal. 3.6-9 were excised completely, because they spoke of the Gospel being 'preached beforehand unto Abraham'

[8] Gal. 5.1.
[9] On this identification see above, p. 69, 70.

and referred to faithful Christians as 'sons of Abraham'.[10] It is probable, too, that Marcion supplied each epistle with a short preface, indicating who the people were to whom it was written, and what were the circumstances of writing. He may also have been responsible for the first chapter-divisions and chapter-headings. But in any case Marcion's collection of St. Paul's Epistles was rather more than just a collection. We should describe it nowadays as the first known 'edition', and say further that it was 'published' at Rome about 150.

The history of the other New Testament books in the early Church was generally similar to that of the Pauline Epistles, although naturally in each instance the details vary.

The four Gospels, for example, may very well have been written originally, as were the Pauline Epistles, for the benefit of particular churches or individuals. But if so, copies of them soon found their way elsewhere. The fact that St. Mark provided the framework for both St. Matthew and St. Luke is clear proof of this. Churches would exchange Gospels just as they did St. Paul's Epistles; and by the second decade of the second century there can have been few churches that did not possess more than one Gospel. Justin Martyr, writing about the middle of the century, describes the public reading of them in the services of the Church: he himself calls them 'Memoirs of the Apostles'—in the plural; but in an adjacent passage he notes that the popular name was 'Gospels'.[11]

So also with the other books. Revelation was addressed, not to one, but to seven churches: I Peter to a number of unspecified churches in no less than five different provinces: James to 'the twelve tribes of the Dispersion'; and The Epistle of Barnabas (included among the books of the New Testament in the great 'Sinai' manuscript in the British Museum) to the writer's 'sons and daughters'—i.e. to Christian men and women generally. All these writings, therefore, were bound to be copied, re-copied, and exchanged, with the result that each separate church came in course of time to possess a library of Christian literature, which was drawn upon for both private and (more especially) public reading.

It was, indeed, the growing tendency to regard the library as primarily a storehouse for the books which were read at the public

[10] On the possibility of Marcion's having excised the last two chapters of Romans see above, p. 52.
[11] Justin, *Apol.*, 1.66,67.

services that seems first to have raised for the members of a church the question, What *ought* we to have in our library? Not all churches, manifestly, would have collected at any given time precisely the same books in their libraries. The better known and more important books, like St. Matthew or Romans, would by the middle of the second century be found almost everywhere. But it was not so with the less known and less important books like Revelation or James or Barnabas.

So long as the books were collected merely in order to form a library no serious problem arose. The presence or absence of a particular book in the library of a particular church would be determined by a variety of considerations: whether or not, for instance, a copy could be easily obtained, or even whether or not the procuring of a copy might be too expensive—for we must remember that book-production in the ancient world was a far more laborious and costly business than it is now, and Christians were for the most part poor people. Immediately, however, it was generally accepted that the primary purpose in adding to a church's library was the provision of additional material for reading in public worship, the whole subject became vastly more complicated.

Together with much else of Jewish origin the primitive Church had taken over the Jewish Bible, or 'the Scriptures' as they were commonly called. These 'Scriptures' were regarded by Christians, no less than by Jews, as the authoritative Word of God; and they were regularly used, as has been pointed out more than once already, to prove the truth of the Christian claim that in 'the things concerning Jesus' God's promises were being fulfilled. But this was by no means all. From the very beginning the regular reading of selected scriptural passages had been a feature of Christian worship. When, therefore, the custom was introduced of reading in the services extracts from Christian writings as well, the inference could hardly be avoided that they, too, were in some sense authoritative, and that they, too, were somehow 'Scripture'. Thus arose the idea of a *corpus* of Christian Scripture to supplement the *corpus* inherited from Judaism, of a 'New' Testament (or 'Covenant') to be set alongside what was henceforth known as the 'Old' Testament, and which, of course, was to be ranked equally as part of 'the Bible'.

For a long time, inevitably, the idea received no formal expression. Each church would read in its services whatever the local leaders thought most suitable from the books in their local library. But no church could remain indefinitely a law unto itself in this matter any more than in others. As ecclesiastical organization developed and the various local churches came more and more to conform to an accepted pattern, the question, 'What *ought* we to have in our library?' (in fact, the question, Which books belong to the New Testament and which do not?) became more pressing. Some standard or rule was essential. For the merely haphazard collection of whatever Christian writings could be come by was plainly not enough.

The answer was found in the making, or drawing up, of a generally recognized Canon.

The word 'canon' originally meant a 'reed'. And because a reed was employed in measuring it came to be used in the sense of a 'measuring-rod' or a 'ruler', and hence in the sense of a 'list' or 'table'. As applied to a list of scriptural books the actual word was not used before the middle of the fourth century. Yet the idea behind it was very much older. It was, in fact, pre-Christian. The Church had started her existence with a ready-made, Jewish, Canon. She was now proposing to add another—to draw up a list of 'New Testament' books to balance the 'Old'. But according to what criterion was she to decide whether a possible claimant for admission to the list should be included or kept outside?

The Church did not at once issue an official pronouncement to settle the question outright. Nor could she have done so even if she had wished, for the simple reason that the necessary machinery did not exist. A solution satisfactory to all had to be hammered out gradually by agreement between one local church and another, and between groups of churches in different regions. This process took some time. And it was not until the beginning of the fifth century that agreement was finally reached.

Looking back over the history of the period as a whole we may say that three main criteria were applied in deciding whether a book was 'canonical' or not. First, there was the authority derived by a book from its author or alleged author: a book attributed to St. Peter, for example, or to some other outstanding figure, stood a much better chance of acceptance than one attributed to Gaius of Derbe, or to someone who was otherwise completely unknown. Second, there was the authority accorded to the book by the Church at large: a book that could be shown to have been accepted by many churches and for many years was obviously in a much stronger position than one accepted by only a few churches and then only recently. And third, there was the authority which accrued to a book from its own inherent worth.

These criteria were never adhered to rigidly as a sort of rule-of-thumb. Sometimes one would weigh more heavily than the others —occasionally, perhaps, exclusively. Sometimes the overriding consideration would be the opinion of a much respected bishop, or the tradition of the leading church in the area. Nor, again, should we be justified in claiming that they were always applied consciously by those who discussed the question. They are rather generalizations, albeit fair enough generalizations, from the evidence taken in its entirety.

So far as we are aware, the first Canon of New Testament books to be drawn up was that of Marcion. Marcion, we noted, published at Rome about 150, not just a collection of St. Paul's Epistles, but an ' edition ' of them—his *Apostolicum*. Concurrently he published also his *Evangelium*, which consisted of a similarly expurgated and altered ' edition ' of St. Luke. And the *Evangelium* and *Apostolicum* together made up the Marcionite Bible. St. Luke, of course, was selected in preference to any other Gospel because being written by a close friend and companion of St. Paul it was thought to reflect most accurately the Pauline point of view. But to suit Marcion's theories it needed even more editorial treatment than St. Paul's Epistles. The first two chapters were cut out completely: so were all but a few words of chapter 3, and most of chapter 4. Thus, the Gospel began, ' In the fifteenth year of the reign of Tiberius Caesar, Pontius Pilate being governor of Judaea, God came down into Capernaum, a city of Galilee, and began to teach on the sabbath days.'[12] In this way Marcion hoped to conceal the unwelcome truth that the Lord had been born and bred a Jew. And the same anti-Jewish bias was discernible in the many alterations elsewhere—e.g. instead of ' It is easier for heaven and earth to pass away than for one tittle of the law to fall '[13] a Marcionite would read ' It is easier for heaven and earth to pass away than for one tittle of the words of the Lord.'

From the orthodox standpoint the provision of a Canon by a heretic for the use of his own followers was not itself a matter of great moment. After Marcion's excommunication the Marcionites

[12] Luke 3.1; 4.31.   [13] Luke 16.17.

became an entirely separate ecclesiastical organization. Their affairs accordingly were no concern of the Church. Nevertheless, the name of Marcion remains a very important one in the history of the New Testament Canon. And this is not so much because he was the first person ever to draw one up, as because the fact that he had done so forced the orthodox to do the same.

The church at Rome seems to have taken action immediately. In the so-called 'Muratorian Fragment' (so called because it was first published by the Italian scholar Muratori in 1740) is preserved a list of books acknowledged at Rome about 170, with a few notes about each. Unfortunately the fragment is mutilated both at the beginning and the end, and there are several passages in it that are obscure. Its witness consequently is incomplete. But of its value in giving an insight into the debates at Rome at the time it was written there can be no doubt.

Our four Gospels are acknowledged, though the lengthy note about St. John implies that some may have been uncertain about it. Likewise Acts is acknowledged. So also are thirteen Pauline Epistles—i.e. our present list excluding Hebrews; but 'there is in circulation,' the writer adds, 'an Epistle to the Laodiceans, and another to the Alexandrians forged under the name of Paul bearing on the heresy of Marcion, and several others which cannot be received into the Catholic Church, for gall ought not to be mixed with honey'. Next came Jude and 'two Epistles bearing the name of John', all of which are 'received'. Then, rather curiously, Wisdom. 'We receive, also,' the writer continues, 'the Revelations of John and Peter only, but some of our number are unwilling that the latter should be read in church.' After this, reference is made to The Shepherd of Hermas as a 'very recent' production, and to certain other writings which are not received. And then the fragment breaks off.

It will be observed that several of our present books are not mentioned—e.g. I Peter and Hebrews. On the other hand, The Revelation of Peter is accepted, although the writer is aware that there is opposition. An explanation of the omissions may be found in the unsatisfactory state of the fragment's text. But of that we cannot be sure. Details apart, however, the major interest for the student of the history of the New Testament Canon lies in the use of the phrase 'received (or not received) in the Catholic Church'.

A few years later St. Irenaeus, bishop of Lyons (*circa* 180-200), in his monumental work *Against Heresies*, approached the question unhesitatingly from the dogmatic angle. It was essential to possess not merely books, but the right books; and the right books, in contradistinction to what the heretics were maintaining, were the books acknowledged by the Church as a whole. In the case of the Gospels, indeed, there was a sort of inner necessity about the four acknowledged :

' It is impossible,' St. Irenaeus writes, ' that the Gospels should be in number either more or less than these. For as there are four quarters of the world in which we live, and four principal winds, and the Church is scattered over all the earth, and the Gospel is the pillar and ground of the Church and the breath of life, it is natural that it should have four pillars breathing immortality and kindling the life of men. Whence it is evident that the Word, the architect of all things, who sits upon the cherubim and holds all things together, when He was made manifest unto men, gave us His Gospel in fourfold form, but held together by one Spirit. . . . For the cherubim had four faces, and their faces are symbols of the dispensation of the Son of God . . . The Gospels therefore agree with them over whom Christ Himself presides.'[14]

And then he goes on to specify the four Gospels to which he is alluding as those of St. Matthew, St. Mark, St. Luke and St. John.

Such language could not have been used unless the standing of these Gospels in the Church was already well established. And subsequently their place was assured. There was general agreement, too, about Acts and the Pauline Epistles, though there were doubts about Hebrews. On the other books opinions fluctuated— thus, the great Alexandrian Biblical scholar, Origen (†255), was doubtful about II and III John, but he accepted The Shepherd of Hermas and The Teaching of the Twelve Apostles.

The position in the early years of the fourth century is well illustrated by the careful statement of Eusebius, bishop of Caesarea from 313 to 339. In a passage professing to ' summarize ' the New Testament writings[15] he divides them into three classes : (1) Recognized

---

[14] Irenaeus, *Adv. Haer.*, 3.11.8.   [15] Eusebius, *Hist. Eccl.*, 3.25.

Books, (2) Disputed Books, and (3) Spurious Books. Among the Recognized Books he reckons the four Gospels, Acts, the Pauline Epistles (including Hebrews), I John, I Peter, and (for the majority) Revelation. Among the Disputed Books, 'which are nevertheless known to most', are 'the so-called Epistle of James', Jude, II Peter, and 'the so-called Second and Third Epistles of John, which may be the work of the evangelist or of some other with the same name'. Among the Spurious Books are listed The Acts of Paul, The Shepherd of Hermas, The Revelation of Peter, The Epistle of Barnabas, The Teaching of the Twelve Apostles, and 'in addition the Revelation of John, if this view prevail, for some reject it, although others count it among the Recognized Books'. The Gospel according to the Hebrews 'in which those of the Hebrews who have accepted Christ especially delight', is added to the Spurious Books as a sort of afterthought. And Eusebius concludes by mentioning certain other writings, such as the Gospels 'of Peter, and Thomas, and Matthias', or Acts, such as those of Andrew and John and the other apostles: these books, he says, 'have never been quoted by the orthodox and they ought not to be reckoned even among the Spurious Books, but shunned as altogether wicked and impious'.

Eusebius here is not quite as clear as might have been wished— e.g. why did he not put Revelation firmly into the 'Disputed' class instead of assigning it variously to the 'Recognized' and 'Spurious' classes? Despite this, however, his statement is of considerable significance. He was, after all, one of the most learned men of his age: he was always extremely careful to be accurate, frequently quoting his authorities at length; and in this instance he is plainly attempting to give, not his personal opinion, but the consensus of opinion in the Church. And from what he says it is apparent that the New Testament Canon as we know it was almost fixed. It was only necessary that the books in the 'Disputed' class should be moved up into the 'Recognized' class for the division between 'canonical' and 'uncanonical' to be permanently distinct.

The first writer to make such a clear-cut distinction was St. Athanasius, bishop of Alexandria. In his 'Easter Letter' on the Canon, written in 367 for the purpose of excluding the large number of apocryphal writings then in circulation, he laid down our present twenty-seven books as alone canonical. In doing so he was followed by others, notably by St. Jerome (†420) and St. Augustine of Hippo (†430), the authority of both of whom was immense. A synod at Carthage in 397, at which St. Augustine himself was present, gave formal sanction to the list. And from then onwards there was no deviation.

By the year 400, therefore, the New Testament Canon was complete.

EPILOGUE

IN THE PROLOGUE we took as our starting-point the maxim 'the New Testament is the Church's Book'. It was there pointed out that this maxim, though often understood to mean no more than that the New Testament is the *possession* of the Church, means primarily (for the New Testament student at least) that the New Testament is the *product* of the Church. And it was pointed out further that when we say that the New Testament is the product of the Church we mean (or should mean), not merely that the individual books were written by members of the Church to meet the needs of the Church, but also that the New Testament, as the New Testament, owes its very existence to the Church, since it was the Church, by its corporate decision, that was responsible for the Canon.

It remains now to draw out the implications of this assertion for the modern reader.

There are some to-day who seem to regard the New Testament as existing, as it were, in its own right. For them it is part of 'the Bible'—something given direct to man by God. As a result, it is invested with an absolute authority: it is appealed to in any argument as the sole touchstone of the truth; and its letter (as interpreted by the individual) is accorded supreme control over the voice of the living Church.

Our studies in the preceding chapters will have shown the essential falsity of this position. There we have watched the infant Church growing and developing, and we have watched the New Testament growing and developing with it. We have seen, for example, how St. Paul wrote letters to deal with particular situations: we have seen how the Gospels gave the facts of the Lord's life which fulfilled the Old Testament prophecies and proved that he was 'the Christ': we have seen, too, how Revelation was addressed to persecuted Christians in order to comfort and encourage them. All the New Testament writers, clearly, were writing from within

155

the Church for the Church's immediate edification and benefit. As was indicated in the Prologue, when they wrote they were not consciously writing Scripture; and they would doubtless have been very surprised if anyone had suggested they were. Whatever, therefore, there may be (and indeed is) of God in the New Testament has been mediated through human channels and communicated ' by divers portions and in divers manners '.

Again, it was the Church, which, after a long and protracted discussion, laid down what books the New Testament should consist of. To-day we read II Peter as part of the New Testament and not Barnabas because the Church has decided we should. Similarly, we read The Revelation of John and not The Revelation of Peter because the Church in the fourth century decided once and for all that the one was Scripture and that the other was not. Consequently, whatever authority attaches to the New Testament is not inherent but rather derived directly from the Church. And any view that would see in the New Testament a self-contained divine deposit, ' coming down out of heaven from God ', is a plain contradiction of the facts.

The New Testament, accordingly, only has meaning when understood against the background of the Church which gave it birth and nourished it to maturity. No doubt it may legitimately be used as a criterion by which to judge the Church, after the manner in which the sixteenth-century Reformers claimed to be using it. No doubt, too, it may legitimately be used as a standard to which the modern Church must conform. But this is only because in canonizing it the ancient Church set it up as a permanent ' rule '. Any attempt to exalt it to a permanent position above the Church, or to use it uncritically as a stick with which to beat the Church on all and every occasion, involves an assumption which in the light of the facts we have been considering is both arbitrary and unjustifiable.

No. The truth is that New Testament and Church belong together—just as much now as in the first four centuries. We have no right to-day either to receive the New Testament, or to interpret it, as of independent authority. It is still, as it always was, and necessarily always must be, nothing less or more than ' the Church's Book '.

BOOKS FOR FURTHER READING

GENERAL

(Arranged in order of size, from the smaller to the greater)

A. M. HUNTER. *Introducing the New Testament.* S.C.M. Press. 1945.

F. B. CLOGG. *An Introduction to the New Testament.* University of London Press. (2nd edit.) 1940.

R. G. HEARD. *An Introduction to the New Testament.* A. and C. Black. 1950.

K. and S. LAKE. *An Introduction to the New Testament.* Christophers. 1938.

A. H. MCNEILE. *Introduction to the Study of the New Testament.* Clarendon Press. 1927.

J. MOFFATT. *An Introduction to the Literature of the New Testament.* T. and T. Clark. (3rd edit.) 1918.

FOR CHAPTER I

F. C. BURKITT. *Christian Beginnings.* University of London Press. 1924. (A succinct, but masterly, survey of Christian origins.)

F. J. FOAKES JACKSON and K. LAKE. *The Beginnings of Christianity.* Volume I. Macmillan. 1920. (An advanced critical survey of the world into which Christianity came and the beginnings of the Christian movement.)

M. DIBELIUS. *From Tradition to Gospel.* Nicholson and Watson. 1934. (A translation of the first serious effort made in modern times to reconstruct the content of the primitive Christian mission preaching.)

C. H. DODD. *The Apostolic Preaching and its Developments.* Hodder and Stoughton. 1936. (A simple and readable statement of the message of the early preachers by one of the leading English New Testament scholars.)

FOR CHAPTERS II AND III

A. D. Nock. *St. Paul.* (Home University Library) Oxford University Press. 1938. (Probably the best short general study of St. Paul obtainable.)

A. Deissmann. *Paul.* Hodder and Stoughton. (2nd edit.) 1926. (A full-length study of the Apostle in his Jewish, Gentile, and Christian, environment.)

A. H. McNeile. *St. Paul.* Cambridge University Press. 1920. (A medium-length study, particularly good in relating the Epistles to their author's life.)

W. M. Ramsay. *St. Paul the Traveller and the Roman Citizen.* Hodder and Stoughton. (18th edit.) 1935. (An eminently readable account by an acknowledged expert in the history and archæology of the world of St. Paul's day.)

K. Lake. *The Earlier Epistles of St. Paul.* Rivingtons. (2nd edit.) 1927. (For the more advanced student. Deals mainly, though not exclusively, with *Thessalonians, Corinthians, Galatians,* and *Romans.*)

G. S. Duncan. *St. Paul's Ephesian Ministry.* Hodder and Stoughton. 1929. (States the case for the Ephesian origin of the 'Captivity' Epistles.)

P. N. Harrison. *The Problem of the Pastoral Epistles.* Clarendon Press. 1921. (States the case for denying the Pauline authorship of these Epistles as they stand.)

A. M. Hunter. *Paul and His Predecessors.* Nicholson and Watson. 1940. (A short examination of St. Paul's debt to 'those who were in Christ' before him.)

W. L. Knox. *St. Paul and the Church of Jerusalem.* Cambridge University Press. 1925. (A detailed study of the events and problems of St. Paul's early career.)

W. L. Knox. *St. Paul and the Church of the Gentiles.* Cambridge University Press. 1939. (A continuation of the previous study into the later period.)

FOR CHAPTER IV

M. Dibelius. *From Tradition to Gospel.* Nicholson and Watson. 1934. (A translation of the first modern investigation of the pre-literary stages of the Gospel tradition.)

B. S. Easton. *The Gospel before the Gospels*. Scribner. 1928. (A critical account of twentieth-century research into the pre-literary stages of the tradition and an estimate of the validity of the methods employed.)

C. F. Burney. *The Poetry of Our Lord*. Clarendon Press. 1925. (A study of the Words of Jesus in the light of Semitic poetic forms.)

T. W. Manson. *The Sayings of Jesus*. S.C.M. Press. 1949. (An examination of the Words of Jesus together with a commentary on them.)

F. C. Burkitt. *The Gospel History and its Transmission*. T. and T. Clark. 1906. (A first-class readable statement of scholarly opinion on the subject in the earlier years of the century.)

W. Sanday (ed.). *Oxford Studies in the Synoptic Problem*. Clarendon Press. 1911. (A collection of essays by various authors, dealing with the literary relationship between the first three Gospels.)

B. H. Streeter. *The Four Gospels*. Macmillan. 1924. (A monumental study of Gospel origins, particularly valuable on the literary side.)

G. D. Kilpatrick. *The Origins of the Gospel according to St. Matthew*. Clarendon Press. 1948. (A detailed study of the origins of a single Gospel.)

A. E. J. Rawlinson. *St. Mark*. (Westminster Commentaries.) Methuen. (4th edit.) 1936. (Probably the best commentary on the English text of any Biblical book available.)

R. H. Lightfoot. *The Gospel Message of St. Mark*. Clarendon Press. 1950. (A succinct and penetrating study of St. Mark's theological purpose as revealed by his choice and ordering of his material.)

J. M. Creed. *The Gospel according to St. Luke*. Macmillan. 1930. (A first-rate commentary on the Greek text with a most valuable Introduction.)

W. F. Howard. *The Fourth Gospel in Recent Criticism and Research*. Epworth Press. (2nd edit.) 1935. (A full account of modern opinion on the subject.)

FOR CHAPTER V

(*a*) W. L. KNOX. *The Acts of the Apostles*. Cambridge University Press. 1948. (An outstandingly successful brief review of the problems involved.)

H. J. CADBURY. *The Making of Luke-Acts*. Macmillan. 1927. (A scholarly study in editorial method.)

F. J. FOAKES JACKSON and K. LAKE. *The Beginnings of Christianity*. Volumes II, IV, and V. Macmillan. 1922-33. (Volume II deals with critical problems: Volume IV is a commentary on the authors' own English translation: Volume V consists of a series of 'additional notes' on particular passages and other matters, which are too lengthy to be included in the commentary.)

(*b*) G. H. RENDALL. *The Epistle of St. James and Judaistic Christianity*. Cambridge University Press. 1927. (A study of the Epistle against its Jewish-Christian background.)

E. G. SELWYN. *The First Epistle of St. Peter*. Macmillan. (2nd edit.) 1947. (A detailed commentary on the Greek text with an extended Introduction—in favour of the Petrine authorship.)

F. W. BEARE. *The First Epistle of Peter*. Blackwell. 1947. (A less detailed Introduction and commentary on the Greek text, with the author's own English translation—against the Petrine authorship.)

(*c*) A. HANSON and R. PRESTON. *The Revelation of St. John the Divine*. S.C.M. Press. 1949. (A simple commentary with Introduction. Most helpful for the beginner.)

E. F. SCOTT. *The Book of Revelation*. S.C.M. Press. 1939. (A study of the book as a whole. Again most helpful for the beginner.)

R. H. CHARLES. *Revelation*. (International Critical Commentaries.) T. and T. Clark. 1920. (An advanced Introduction, with commentary on the Greek text.)

A. FARRER. *A Rebirth of Images*. Dacre Press. 1949. (A subtle study of the structure and symbolism of *Revelation* in the light of St. John's Hebrew and Jewish antecedents.)

INDEX OF REFERENCES

GENERAL INDEX

171